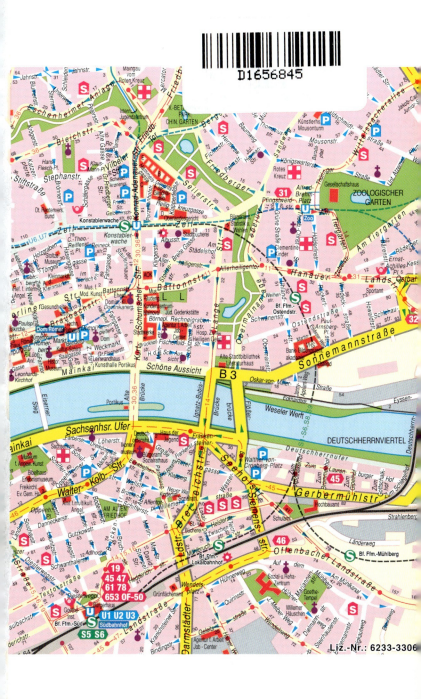

Kristiane Müller-Urban/Eberhard Urban
Translated by Annett Hartmann M.A.

Frankfurt on Foot

Strolls and Hikes
through the Metropolis on the Main

SOCIETÄTS**VERLAG**

The details and information provided for in this book have been recently researched. Although they have been checked carefully before edition, we must point out that telephone numbers, business hours and other data might change from time to time.

Signs
and their meanings

🅢 S-Bahn
🅤 Underground
🚋 Trams
🚌 Bus lines

 Kids' fun guaranteed

Photo page 2: Römer, historical town hall

All rights reserved • Societäts-Verlag
© 2006 Frankfurter Societäts-Druckerei GmbH
Art direction and design: Nicole Proba, Societäts-Verlag
Coverdesign: Katja Holst, Frankfurt am Main
Cover: Michael Wicander, Frankfurt am Main
http://www.skyline-frankfurt.com/
Printers: Jütte-Messedruck Leipzig GmbH
Printed in Germany 2006
ISBN-10: 3-7973-1013-7
ISBN-13: 978-3-7973-1013-2

Content

Preface 7

Frankfurt is full of peculiarities –
Accompanying Goethe
through history 8

**How could come that anyone
was not from Frankfurt! –**
Friedrich Stoltze is taking you
through Alt-Frankfurt and
Sachsenhausen 18

Culture for everybody –
Museums' Bank and other
museums in Frankfurt's city 28

Honouring the Saviour –
Pilgrimage for true and
non-believers to churches,
monasteries and the cathedral 46

The despised alley –
The Rothschild family
and the Jewish Frankfurt 54

Frankfurt has so many goods –
Shopping in Frankfurt's city 66

Beautifully arranged plantations –
The Plantation Ring, the
Senckenberg Museum of Natural
History, Palm Garden and Zoo

78

Behind Frankfurt the sea –
Accompanying Robert
Gernhardt through
Frankfurt's Green Belt 90

Sex & crime in the city –
The girl Rosemarie takes you
through the night

104

Service –
City map, addresses and
offers, boats, busses and trams 116

Index of Photographs 126

Preface

Frankfurt on the Main is at the same time a modern and a time-honoured city, hometown for old-established Frankfurters as well as people from all over the world. Due to its favoured geographical situation near the river and in the centre of far-reaching trade routes leading to the west and the east, the south and the north, Frankfurt had already become a pivot of Germany and Europe in the early Middle Ages.

Until today, the town has conserved its status of a hub. Thanks to the airport and the railway network, it has even become a centre not only of the continent, but of the whole world.

In Frankfurt, craft and trade have always been prospering, industry and banking followed. These are the right surroundings for science and research, poetry, fine and other arts.

Walkers and strollers will discover what Frankfurt has to offer in terms of sights and peculiarities from past and recent times. When walking through the "city of the scyscrapers", one passes its streets and alleys, but also the rich nature in its core as well as the Green Belt that is surrounding Frankfurt.

Some people jet to Paris or New York for shopping. But you will find Tiffany & Co also in Frankfurt. In lifestyle and savoir-vivre, for modest and luxury pleasures – Frankfurt is the right city for every taste, by day and night. That is something this book, a true companion on all ways, is going to prove.

We would like to thank everybody who has given advice and support for the preparation of this book.

The authors and the publishers

Frankfurt is full of peculiarities
Accompanying Goethe through history

The poet who created this motto had already discovered the town as a child, by walking. Following his tracks, even children will have fun as history comes to life.

Accompanying Goethe through history

The walk through history, which is also exciting for children, starts at **Hauptwache** with its underground station, where many regional and underground trains from all directions stop. It is a walk of about one kilometre.

The Hauptwache, according to Goethe "properly built and well situated", was a military building of the town's police station, finished in 1729/1730. Rebellious citizens were also incarcerated here. Students and young workmen stormed the Hauptwache in 1833. Today, the baroque building serves as a restaurant, café and bar.

The eye turns to the church **Katharinenkirche**, built in 1681, where Goethe was confirmed. To the right of the church, the way leads to Großer Hirschgraben via Kleiner Hirschgraben. That's where the **Goethe-House** is situated; the place where Johann Wolfgang was born on August 28, 1749. In 16 rooms, spread over four floors, the visitor finds antique furniture and plenty of pictures, illustrating Goethe's domes-

Goethe-House;
Previous pages:
Historical Museum

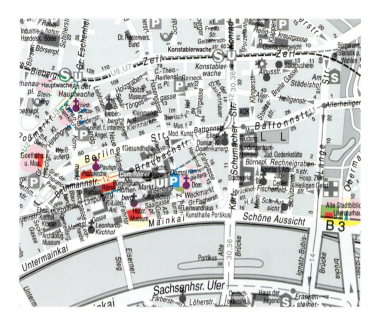

tic surroundings during his growing up. Goethe left Frankfurt as a young man, but time and again he returned to his hometown when he was on one of his travels. After a full and active life, he died in Weimar on March 22, 1832.

The museum that is devoted to the poet, showing Goethe's work as well as several special exhibitions, is very nearby. The institution Freies Deutsches Hochstift does not only combine the Goethe memorial and the museum; it is a research institute that keeps about 40,000 manuscripts. The library, consisting of approximately 120,000 books, is open to the public.

Coming from the Goethe-House and the Goethe-Museum and walking some steps further,

> **Frankfurt Goethe-Museum and Goethe-House**
>
> Großer Hirschgraben 23–25
> 60311 Frankfurt am Main
> Phone 069/13 88 00
> Fax 069/13 88 02 22
> info@goethehaus-frankfurt.de
> www.goethehaus-frankfurt.de
>
> Business hours
> Sun – Fri and holidays 10 am – 5.30 pm,
> Sat 10 am – 6 pm
> Admission
> € 5.–, reduced € 3.–, families € 8.–, children from 6 years on € 1.50

all along the street Großer Hirschgraben, you will get to Berliner Straße. Follow this street on the left hand side until the pedestrian crossing. To your right, you can already see the church **Paulskirche**. Its construction was started in 1787, and it was "built after the most modern style", how Goethe used to say. In the year 1848, during the revolution, the church was used by the delegates of the first all-German parliament, the National Assembly.

Crossing Braubachstraße, you will come to the **Römerberg**. Whereas the citizens of Frankfurt call it their "cosy parlour" ("gud stubb"), Goethe said it

was a nice place to go for a pleasant walk. The square is dominated by the central Fountain of Justice and its goddess of justice. As the goddess is not blindfolded, she can have a critical look at the town hall. The historical town hall consists of several time-honoured buildings, the oldest mentioned in 1322 for the first time. It is named "**Römer**" after the middle building with its three-stepped pediments. The Kaisersaal of the Römer, the "emperors' hall", shows larger-than-life paintings of German emperors, which had already impressed Goethe.

Opposite the Römer, the wide square is bordered by a row of pretty half-timbered houses. This eastern row is a reproduction of the six historical buildings that had been shaped after the medieval model before the First World War. The

Eastern row at Römerberg

cathedral Kaiserdom is rising up behind the half-timbered houses. It is the place where, in the past, the German kings and emperors were elected and crowned. In the archaeological garden in front of the cathedral, the oldest excavations stem from Roman times. The coronation ceremonies were held on the Römerberg and in the Römer. In "Poetry and Truth", Goethe draws a vivid picture of the several events on the occasion of the election and crowning of Joseph II. in 1764.

Southbound, the Römerberg is bordered by the church Alte Nikolaikirche and the **Historical Museum**, which is accommodated in one modern building as well as in several historical buildings; among them the Bernus and Burnitz houses, which date

Charles the Great in front of the Historical Museum

from the 18th and 19th century, the chapel Saalhofkapelle from the 12th century and the tower Rententurm, which goes back to the 15th century. The enormous statue of Charles the Great is situated at its entrance. According to a folk tale, he once had to flee from the Saxons to the Main, where a white hind appeared to show him and his Franconians a ford through the river. The town received its name from this moment in its history (Frankfurt = the ford of the Franconians), and it was already mentioned for the first time in 794. Finally, Charles the Great defeated the Saxons and let them settle down on the south bank, in Sachsenhausen (meaning: the home of the Saxons).

The town's prehistory reaches back to the Stone Age, 4000 years ago, and since Charles the Great, it has been a central place in Germany and Europe. In the Historical Museum, Frankfurt's history is illustrated by means of pictures, documents, furniture, textiles, weapons and other exhibits.

The museum includes the Children's Museum, called Kindermuseum, which easily explains historical knowledge to children.

The Museum of Comical Art, "Caricatura/Museum für Komische Kunst", belongs to the Historical Museum, too. It mainly shows the work of Robert Gernhardt, Chlodwig Poth, Hans Traxler, Friedrich Karl Waechter and Bern Pfarr, all coming from the New Frankfurt School, Neue Frankfurter Schule, and it is designed to make the visitor smile, laugh and think about.

Children´s Museum
Saalgasse 19 (Römerberg)
60311 Frankfurt am Main
Phone 0 69/21 23 55 99
Fax 0 69/21 23 07 02
info.historisches-
museum@stadt-frankfurt.de
www.historisches-
museum.frankfurt.de

Business hours
Tue, Thu – Sun 10 am –
5 pm, Wed 10 am – 8 pm
Admission
€ 4.–, reduced € 2.–

Caricatura
from fall 2007 on:
Braubachstr. 30 – 34
60311 Frankfurt am Main

The way back to Hauptwache and the station continues straight on, over Römerberg, crossing Braubachstraße, all along Neue Kräme and Liebfrauenstraße, and it is about 600 metres long.

Only a few steps take you from the Historical Museum to the Mainkai, the quay of the Main. The excursion boats of the shipping company Primus start here. The footbridge Eiserner Steg, meaning the iron footbridge, goes over the river, to Sachsenhausen. When Goethe was living here, he could not use that bridge, for it was only built in 1869.

House of Literature, the former municipal library

Those who want to walk a bit more, can turn to the left, passing the hall court, Saalhof, of the Historical Museum. Goethe is right: "On the side of the Main, the Saalhof is a rather regular and attractive building." The way on the riverbank leads you under the bridge Alte Brücke, and after 900 metres it goes up to the **House of Literature**, the Literaturhaus, climbing up the steps of the bridge Ignatz-Bubis-Brücke.

The House of Literature was built as a public library between 1820 and 1825. However, the bombs of the Second World War only spared the classicistic entrance hall with its columns. Meanwhile, the destroyed building has been restored and attached to the vestibule, the building now being again "that place equipped and enriched with wise treasures, perfectly designed by its architects and situated in the most beautiful setting." (Goethe)

Return
O Tram, 14
   Stop Hospital zum Heiligen Geist
   to Ostendstraße, change to
O S-Bahn S1-S6, S8, S9
   to Hauptwache or Hauptbahnhof (main station)

How could come that anyone was not from Frankfurt!
Friedrich Stoltze is taking you through Alt-Frankfurt and Sachsenhausen

Most people know him as a humorous regional writer. However, Stoltze was also a sharp satirist, a committed journalist, and an honest fighter for freedom and a democratic Germany.

Friedrich Stoltze is taking you through Alt-Frankfurt and Sachsenhausen

Many Frankfurters, who might know only a few poems by Goethe, like quoting verses by Friedrich Stoltze, such as: "There is no place in the wide world / I like as much as my Frankfurt / And it will never get into my mind / How could come that anyone was not from Frankfurt!" Within one verse of this Frankfurt poem, the newcomer finds his certain comfort: "Even a naturalised will always come from here."

Stoltze was also familiar with the historical buildings we visited when we had been strolling with Goethe.

The way from **Hauptwache**, at the same time station for many underground and regional trains from all directions, to the Stoltze-Museum and until the banks of the Main is about 1.5 kilometres long. Nowadays used as a restaurant, café and bar, the baroque Hauptwache was originally a military building of the town's police station, which was also used as a prison. Here, the young revolutionists who took part in the attack of the guards in 1833, were incarcerated. Stoltze's beloved and

Hauptwache;
Previous pages: Alt-Sachsenhausen

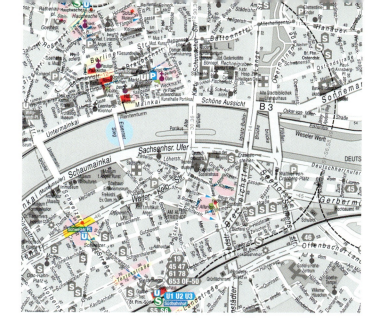

three-years-older sister, Annett, plotted their rescue. The enterprise failed, Annett was imprisoned, and after the birth of her son, received in free love, she had to stay in prison for four weeks. The ardent Republican Annett was Stoltze's idol, she had encouraged him to become a writer.

Opposite the Hauptwache, there is the church **Katharinenkirche**, where Stoltze, who was a Protestant, got married to the Catholic Marie Messenzahl, who was in her third pregnancy, in 1849. At that time, such a "mixed marriage" was rather unusual.

Behind Katharinenkirche, just going through the next alley, you find the square **Friedrich-Stoltze-Platz** with the

Friedrich Stoltze Monument

Stoltze-Museum

poet's monument. His flowing mane makes him look like Karl Marx.

The street Bleidenstraße borders the square to the south. If you follow the street to the left, you will get to the church Liebfrauenkirche, whose construction was started in the 14th century. Continuing straight on, you will get to the street Töngesgasse, where the bank Sparkasse Frankfurt has established the **Stoltze-Museum** in a listed Renaissance stair tower. It shows Stoltze's life, from November 21, 1816 to March 28, 1891, and his work as an author, editor and publisher of the newspapers "Krebbel-Zeitung" and "Frankfurter Latern", in which he lit the light of the enlightenment.

Stoltze-Museum
Töngesgasse 34 – 36
60311 Frankfurt am Main
Phone 0 69/26 41 40 06
Fax 0 69/26 41 40 26
petra.breitkreuz@
fraspa1822.de

www.fraspa1822.de
Business hours
Mon, Tue, Thu, Fri
9.30 am – 5 pm,
Wed 9.30 am – 8 pm
Admission free

The street Töngesgasse ends at the so-called Staufenmauer, the remains of the town wall from the early 13th century. A few metres before the wall, the street Hasengasse leads to the right. After you have crossed Berliner Straße and come to the cathedral, the "Dom", the Hasengasse changes its name into Domstraße. Friedrich Stoltze was born in the middle of that maze of alleys all around the cathedral on November 21, 1816, being the son of the proprietor of the restaurant Gasthaus zum Rebstock, "one of the main pubs of the then demagogues in Frankfurt." The house does not exist any more. The writer notes about his birthplace, "the Rewestock, my home, laid close to the Pathorn", the latter referring to the rectory tower, the tower of the cathedral.

His father wanted Stoltze to become a merchant. He worked in a silk shop in Lyon, but then, he went to Thuringia, where he developed educational skills – "the first class, that is the teacher, / the quiet patron of the mind's empire." However, Stoltze did not want to be quiet. He enthusiastically welcomed the revolution in 1848 as well as the parliament, that met in the church Paulskirche. Only a few steps take you from the cathedral to the Römerberg with the historical town hall **Römer** and the square Paulsplatz with the church **Paulskirche**.

St. Paul's Church, Paulskirche

The panoramic picture "Zug der Volksvertreter auf dem Weg in die Paulskirche" (The procession of the people's representatives towards St. Paul's Church) was painted in 1990 by Johannes Grützke and stretches all around the core of its covered walk. It is three metres high and 32 metres long. Friedrich Stoltze would have liked the picture for its realistic, sometimes rather rough style.

In 1849, the parliament's longing for a democratic and unified Germany failed mainly due to the Prussians. Many brave men and women did not want to give up, and participated in the armed struggle. Stoltze became a volunteer soldier in the Palatinate. "I am wearing the dress of the free soldier / and I am not taking rulers' pay, / I have sworn the oath of allegiance / on the banner Black-Red-Gold." However, the rebellion there was put down, above all by Prussian soldiers.

Back in Frankfurt, Stoltze unfurled his publishing activities, heaping scorn on the Prussian Bismarck, who was of nearly the same age, and his politics. Stoltze's attacks culminated after Prussia had occupied and annexed the free Frankfurt in 1866. Therefore, he had to emigrate, but he did not stop fighting. "You might pray, but I cannot! / Praying cannot rescue us, / With hands folded / people will never break their chains…"

The passage from Römerberg to the Main is called Fahrtor. To the left, the complex of the buildings of the Historical Museum can be seen. The name of the tower in the corner is Rententurm. In here, Annett

Tower, Rententurm

had to serve her hard prison sentence, which finally caused her early death on November 17, 1840. She was just 27 years old.

In the Historical Museum, there is the "Historix", a cider pub with an integrated **Cider-Museum** and a Stoltze bust. That leads us to the "Stöffche", as poets and Frankfurters call their cider. Nowadays, the right name for this drink is Ebbelwei, although elsewhere other spellings might exist. "Who does not like that stuff, / I cannot help feeling sorry for! / Nothing of this world / gives us such a pleasure."

In all quarters of Frankfurt, that stuff gives the Schoppepetzer, as the cider drinkers are called, a lot of pleasure. **Sachsenhausen** is said to be the Ebbelwei stronghold. Of course, they also serve other drinks apart from cider. A stroll through the quarter on the southern bank of the Main – Dribbdebach, meaning "on the other side of the stream", seen from Frankfurt, which is also called Hibbdebach, meaning "on this side of the stream" – starts with the crossing of the Main, using the footbridge Eiserner Steg, which was built in 1869.

Those who saunter all over the maze of alleys with its half-timbered buildings, Ebbelwei pubs and other pubs and restaurants,

Footbridge, Eiserner Steg

will have a walk of about two kilometres. Satisfy your hunger with small titbits, such as Handkäs mit Musik, which is cheese made from sour milk and onions to go with, Rindswurst (beef sausage) or frankfurter; or, if you are really hungry, you can eat Scheufelchen, a local speciality, or Rippchen mit Kraut, pork ribs with cabbage. The Ebbelwei will quench your thirst. Usually, the pubs and restaurants open in the late morning.

Coming from the footbridge Eiserner Steg, the way leads to the left. Turn right behind the bridge Alte Brücke onto the street Große Rittergasse, here you will pass the House of the German Order, the Deutschordenshaus, and the House of Youth, the Haus der Jugend. After having passed the tower Kuhhirtenturm from the time around 1490, the way goes straight into **Alt-Sachsenhausen**. Turning right, onto Kleine Rittergasse and from there taking the next alley to the left, called Klappergasse, one gets to the statue of Mrs Rauscher. Rauscher also is the name of the young Ebbelwei, and it can be compared to the fermenting new wine called Federweißer. The two of them, woman and wine, have their own song: "Mrs Rauscher from the Klappergaß, she has a big bump on her nut. / Whether it comes from the Rauscher or from her husband, will be found out by the police." If you rest in front of the monument and want to ruminate where her big bump might stem from, she will spit water at you.

The street Klappergasse leads onto Dreieichstraße, and some steps to the right will take you to the New Rampart, Neuer Wall, and the square Affentorplatz with its two former guard and customs buildings. The buildings, "Affentorhäuser", were built from 1810 to 1811 on the site of the medieval gate Aschaffenburger Tor.

Neuer Wall becomes Wallstraße, and from there, on the left hand, the streets Abtgässchen and Martin-May-Straße lead the strollers through Sach-

Monument to Mrs Rauscher

senhausen onto Textorstraße, leading right to Schweizer Straße. From the station Südbahnhof and from the square Schweizer Platz you can make your journey back to Hibbdebach.

Small choice of Ebbelwei pubs in Sachsenhausen

Zum Eichkatzerl
(To the Squirrel)
Dreieichstr. 29

Klaane Sachsehäuser
(The Small Saxon)
Neuer Wall 11

Germania
Textorstr. 16

Fichtekränzi
(The Pine Wreath)
Wallstr. 5

Zum gemalten Haus
(To the Painted House)
Schweizer Str. 67

Return
O Underground U1, U2, U3
    Stop Südbahnhof or Schweizer Platz to Hauptwache

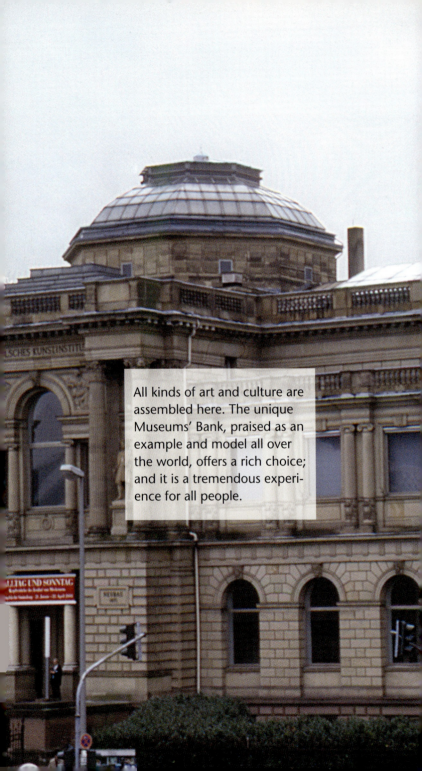

All kinds of art and culture are assembled here. The unique Museums' Bank, praised as an example and model all over the world, offers a rich choice; and it is a tremendous experience for all people.

Culture for everybody
Museums' Bank and other museums in Frankfurt's city

Museums' Bank

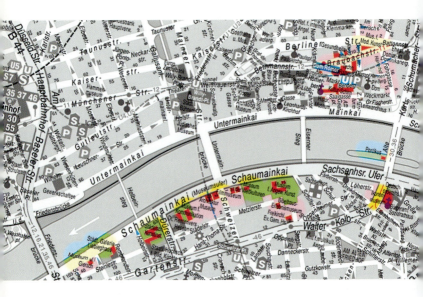

Around 50 museums can be visited in Frankfurt. A dozen museums – which are not only exhibition halls, but locations of various events, also for children – are situated on the southern bank of the Main, from Schaumainkai to the bank of Sachsenhausen, all lined up one after the other over a stretch of about 1.7 kilometres. The idea of the Museums' Bank, as well as many other cultural places and activities, goes back to one of the most important contemporary cultural politicians, Hilmar Hoffmann. He had been town councillor for culture in Frankfurt for 20 years, and his work can be summarised by the slogan "culture for everybody".

From the main station, the Hauptbahnhof, the trams 12, 16 and 21, as well as the bus

"Lastenträger" (Bearer of the Burden),
sculpture by Constantin Meunier, 1893;
previous pages: The Städel Art Institute
and Municipal Gallery

line 46 cross the bridge Friedensbrücke; you must get off at the stop Stresemannallee / Gartenstraße. The sculpture "Lastenträger" (Bearer of the Burden) by Constantin Meunier from the year 1893, marks the beginning of the Museums' Bank.

After a few steps, you have already reached the **Museum Giersch**. It is a Karin and Carlo Giersch foundation, and it is devoted to changing exhibitions of great artists and important subjects of art. The exhibits are selected from international museums, galleries and private collections. As all works of art are presented in a brilliant way, these exhibitions are always important events.

Museum Giersch
Schaumainkai 83
60596 Frankfurt am Main
Phone 0 69/63 30 41 28
Fax 0 69/63 30 41 44
museum-giersch@
schaumainkai.de

www.museum-giersch.de
Business hours
Tue – Fri 12 pm – 7 pm, Sat and Sun 11 am – 5 pm
Admission
€ 4.–, reduced € 2.–

In the garden of the museum, the statues of Athena, Marsyas and the "Ariadne auf dem Panther" (Ariadne on the Panther) already give a hint on one of the most important European collections of sculptures that is shown here, in the museum **Liebieg-**

"Ariadne auf dem Panther" (Ariadne on the Panther),
sculpture by Johann Heinrich Danecker, 1814

haus. The original of Ariadne, the famous work of the sculptor Johann Heinrich Danecker from 1814, as well as the originals of other classical figures can be seen in the museum of Ancient Sculpture, "Alter Plastik". The collection reaches from the Egypt of the Pharaohs, the Ancient Greece and Rome over the Middle Ages, Renaissance, Baroque and Rococo up to the 19th century, complemented by art works from India and China.

Museum Liebieghaus **Museum of Ancient Sculpture** Schaumainkai 71 60596 Frankfurt am Main Phone 0 69/21 23 86 15 Fax 0 69/21 23 07 01	liebieghaus@stadt-frankfurt.de www.liebieghaus.de Business hours Tue – Fri 10 am – 5 pm, Wed 10 am – 8 pm Admission € 4.–, reduced € 2.50

The Städel – Städel Art Institute and Municipal Gallery – presents one of the most important international art collections. The paintings from the Middle Ages to the present time colourfully illustrate the history of arts. Let's mention at least a few of the painters, some of them lived in Frank-

"Die Kreuzerhöhung" (The raising of the Cross), painting by Adam Elsheimer, after 1600

furt, out of the great variety of artists. Jan van Eyck (around 1390 – 1441) and his brother Hubert are considered to be the founders of panel painting on wood and canvas; Jan's beautiful Lucca-Madonna can be seen here. Hans Holbein the Eldest (1465 – 1524) painted the "Madonna des Bügermeisters Jakob Meyer zum Hasen" (Madonna of the mayor Jakob Meyer to the Rabbit). One altar piece and a charming, delicate Venus stem from Lucas Cranach the Eldest (1472 – 1553). Matthias Grünewald (around 1460 – 1528), the expressionist of his time, is present with some altar pieces. Adam Elsheimer (1578 – 1610), who was famous in Rome as "Frankfurt painter", influenced many artists, among them Rubens and Rembrandt. In the Städel, one can have a look at the lay altar by Elsheimer, with many single paintings and a variety of other pieces. Of course, the Städel shows master pieces of Rubens and Rembrandt, Jan Vermeer, Frans Hals and several other painters from Flanders and Holland. Famous Italians, for example Tiepolo and Canaletto, too. "Goethe in der römischen Campagna"

"Goethe in der römischen Campagna" (Goethe in the Roman Campagne), painting by Johann Heinrich Wilhelm Tischbein, 1786/87

(Goethe in the Roman Campagne), painted in 1786/87 by Johann Heinrich Wilhelm Tischbein, is one of the best-known paintings in the Städel.

Important paintings by Joseph Anton Koch, Caspar David Friedrich, Carl Blechen and other Romantics, like the members of the painter association Nazarener from the 19th century, are also present. From the second half of the 19th century onwards Jacob Becker and his Städel pupils, among them many artists from the painters' colony Kronberg around the great artist Anton Burger, preferred the Realism, as it was propagated by Gustave Courbet. Courbet, a friend of the Kronbergers, had also stayed in Frankfurt, painting in the town and its surroundings.

In the last third of the 19th century, Realism turned into Impressionism. The Städel, always open to new and modern tendencies, bought important pieces by Manet, Monet, Renoir,

"Blick auf Frankfurt" (View of Frankfurt on the Main), painting by Gustave Courbet, 1858/59

Degas, van Gogh and other impressionists, as well as by their German colleagues Corinth and Liebermann.

Influenced by the expressive art of van Gogh, the expressionists used enhanced forms and colours from the beginning of the 20th century. The museum in Frankfurt shows the work of Otto Dix, Erich Heckel, Ernst-Ludwig Kirchner, Paula Modersohn-Becker, Otto Mueller, Emil Nolde, Karl Schmidt-Rottluff, Franz Marc, August Macke, Alexej von Jawlensky, Paul Klee, Lyonel Feininger and other expressionists. The work of Max Beckmann, who lived in Frankfurt since 1915 and who was a professor at the Städel school, is presented to a large extent. Like other artists, he was slandered and pursued by the Nazis since 1933, and then went into exile.

After the Nazis had stolen 500 paintings of Modern Art from the museum in 1936, in order to burn them as "degenerate art" or to sell them abroad, the museum managed to purchase pieces by Willi Baumeister, Max Beckmann, Max Ernst, Fernand Léger, Henri Matisse, Ernst Wilhelm Nay, Pablo Picasso and others after 1945, which has enabled the museum to show its visitors a valid overall picture of the arts.

Master pieces of the varied contemporary art are mainly shown in the new annex building. Bernhard Heisig, Anselm Kiefer, Markus Lüpertz, A.R. Penck, Sigmar Polke and Gerhard Richter are worth mentioning.

The collection of graphic arts consists of about 100,000 sketches and prints from the Middle Ages until now, and it belongs to the most important collections in Germany. In its exhibition hall, parts of the holdings are shown in form of changing exhibitions.

Städel Art Institute
Schaumainkai 63
60596 Frankfurt am Main
Phone 0 69/6 05 09 80
Fax 0 69/61 01 63
info@staedelmuseum.de
www.staedelmuseum.de

Business hours
Tue, Fri – Sun 10 am – 5 pm,
Wed and Thu 10 am – 9 pm
Admission
€ 6.–, reduced € 5.–,
family ticket € 10.–

At the entrance of the **Museum of Communication**, a technical-fantastical horseman from the time when the telephone had not been invented yet, the so-called "Pre-Bell man 5 000 000 B.C. – 1860 A. D.", created 1990 by the Corean multimedia artist Nam June Paik welcomes the visitors.

The history and the present forms of communication – from the bush drum over the stagecoach until the communications satellite – are vividly illustrated by an abundance of exhibits, complemented by video terminals and interactive models. An art exhibition with works dedicated to communication completes the show of the great museum.

Museum of Communication
Schaumainkai 55
60596 Frankfurt am Main
Phone 0 69/6 06 00
Fax 0 69/6 06 06 66
mk-frankfurt@mspt.de
www.museumsstiftung.de

Business hours
Tue – Fri 9 am – 5 pm, Sat, Sun, holidays 11 am – 7 pm
Admission
€ 2.–, children from 6 years on € 1.–

The **German Architecture Museum**, Deutsches Architekturmuseum (DAM), which is the first of its kind in Europe, was established by Oswald Mathias Ungers, being a house within a house. The exciting permanent and temporary exhibitions focus on the past and the future of the international art of construction and urban development. Even children will find the demonstration "From the primeval hut to the skyscraper" interesting.

German Architecture Museum
Schaumainkai 43
60596 Frankfurt am Main
Phone 0 69/21 23 88 44
Fax 0 69/21 23 63 86
www.dam-online.de
info.dam@stadt-frankfurt.de
Business hours
Tue – Sun 11 am – 6 pm,
Wed 11 am – 8 pm
Admission
€ 6.–, reduced € 3.–

Film poster by Klaus Dill, who has received the German film award
"Filmband des Deutschen Filmpreises" in gold for his poster art

Right next to it, you can visit the first **Film Museum** of the world. Here, you will experience how pictures learned to walk. The prehistory and early history of the film is one part of the museum, film technology another. Visitors become stars in original film settings, where Humphrey Bogart and other famous actors played once. Carefully planned special exhibitions deal with real stars, film directors, decorators, and painters of film posters. After they have been shown in Frankfurt, they often go on tour around the world.

A rich archive and a film library turn the museum into a research institute. And, of course, there is a cinema with a programme that pleases all film fans.

> **German Film Museum**
> Schaumainkai 41
> 60596 Frankfurt am Main
> Phone 0 69/21 23 88 30
> Fax 0 69/21 23 78 81
> info@deutsches-
> filmmuseum.de
>
> www.deutsches-
> filmmuseum.de
> Business hours
> Tue, Thu, Fri, Sun 10 am –
> 5 pm, Wed 10 am – 8 pm,
> Sat 2 pm – 8 pm
> Admission
> € 2.50, reduced € 1.30

The **Museum of World Cultures** has the motto "Foreign ways – different perspectives" and invites its visitors to cross the borders of their own cultural horizons. Special exhibitions are shown in the house Schaumainkai 29, where changing exhibitions present the numerous treasures of the museum, consisting of about 65,000 pieces of art and other objects from Oceania, Australia, South-East Asia, America, Africa and Europe.

Ethiopian ancestor stones in the garden of the Museum of World Cultures

The **Gallery 37** is situated in the house number 37 and performs special exhibitions – the work of American Indian, Latin American, African, Australian, Oceanian and Indonesian contemporary artists, who until now have hardly been noticed by art museums.

Museum of World Cultures/Gallery 37
Schaumainkai 29–37
60594 Frankfurt am Main
Phone 0 69/21 23 59 13
Fax 0 69/21 23 07 04
museum-weltkulturen@-stadt-frankfurt.de
www.mdw-frankfurt.de
www.journal-ethnologie.de

Business hours
Tue, Thu, Fri, Sun 10 am – 5 pm, Wed 10 am – 8 pm, Sat 2 pm – 8 pm
Admission
Museum € 3.60, reduced € 2.–; Gallery € 3.10, reduced € 1.10; Combiticket € 4.60, reduced € 2.60; last Sat in month Donation Day/admission free

The architect Richard Meier erected an exemplary construction for the Museum of Applied Arts, right next to the Villa Metzler from 1804. Highly approved special exhibitions and selected pieces from its collection, which contains more than 30,000 objects from Europe, East Asia, and the Islamic countries, including book and writing arts as well as design, transform the visit into an event.

Museum of Applied Arts
Schaumainkai 17
60594 Frankfurt am Main
Phone 0 69/21 23 40 37
Fax 0 69/21 23 07 03
info.angewandte-kunst@stadt-frankfurt.de
www.museumfuerange-wandtekunst.frankfurt.de

Business hours
Tue, Thu–Sun 10 am – 5 pm, Wed 10 am – 9 pm
Admission
€ 5.–, reduced € 2.50; last Sat in month admission free

The park at the Museum for Applied Arts, a popular lawn and playing field, extends towards the south until Metzlerstraße, where the **House of the Bible** has been established as a museum, which is a real "World of Discovery". Here, the book of the books and the biblical world can be experienced – by means of a boat from the time of Jesus, a nomad's tent, and other exhibits, but also through modern multimedia presentations. The House of the Bible is equally exciting for the old and the young, for believers and non-believers.

**House of Bible –
World of Discovery**
Metzlerstr. 19
60594 Frankfurt am Main
Phone 0 69/66 42 65 25
Fax 0 69/66 42 65 26
info@bibelhaus-frankfurt.de
www.bibelhaus-frankfurt.de

Business hours
Tue 9 am – 12, Wed, Thu
3 pm – 8 pm, Fri 3 pm – 6 pm,
Sat, Sun 2 pm – 6 pm
Admission
€ 5.–, reduced € 4.–,
families € 11.–

The Icon Museum in the baroque building of the German Order, Deutschordenshaus, at the bridge Alte Brücke forms the eastern border of the Museums' Bank. In 1988, Dr. Jörgen Schmidt-Voigt donated 800 icons to the town. Meanwhile, the collection has been

Church Elisabethkirche, part of the house of the German Order, Deutschordenshaus

extended to 1000 paintings of devotions. Also sculptures, blessing crosses, breast crosses, church equipment, church textiles and Ethiopian magic rolls are part of the exhibition. Contemporary artists show their religious work in special exhibitions.

Icon Museum Frankfurt Foundation Dr. Schmidt-Voigt
Brückenstr. 3–7
60594 Frankfurt am Main
Phone 069/21 23 62 62
Fax 069/21 23 99 68
info.ikonen-museum@stadt-frankfurt.de
www.ikonenmuseumfrankfurt.de
Business hours
Tue–Sun 10 am – 5 pm,
Wed 10 am – 8 pm
Admission
€ 3.–, reduced € 2.–,
last Sat in month
admission free

Return
O Bus line 36
Stop Elisabethstraße to Konstablerwache, change to S-Bahn or underground to different directions

Those who have time and mood to continue the cultural trip, or to complete it another day, can do another kilometre of walking. Crossing the bridge Alte Brücke, you will get to the island Maininsel, where the exhibition hall Portikus is situated. It is financed by the Karin and Carlo Giersch Foundation (Museum Giersch), showing new positions of international art since 2006. The Portikus is part of the Städel School, the University of Fine Arts.

Portikus
Alte Brücke/Maininsel
60311 Frankfurt am Main
Phone 069/21 99 87 60
Fax 069/21 99 87 61
info@portikus.de
www.portikus.de
Business hours
Tue–Sun 11 am – 6 pm
Admission free

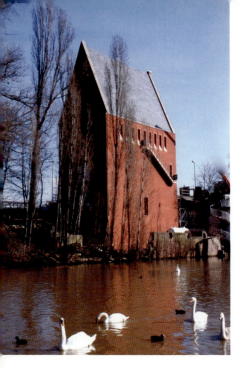

Portikus, the new exhibition hall

On the other bank of the Main, the street Fahrgasse leads, half to the left, into town. On both sides, the alley is skirted by antique shops and art galleries – similar to the street Braubachstraße, which is branching off to the left.

The huge Museum of Modern Art rises between Braubachstraße, Berliner Straße and Domstraße. It is a creation of Hans Hollein, an architect from Vienna. The house is called "Tortenstück", piece of cake, because of its triangular ground-plan, and it shows international modern art from 1960 on. Some of the names underline the importance of that museum: Andy Warhol, Tom Wesselmann, Roy Lichtenstein, Claes Oldenburg, Robert Rauschenberg, Joseph Beuys, Nam June Paik, Mario Merz, Hanne Darboven, Katharina Fritsch, Julian Schnabel. The exhibits and newly bought pieces of art are presented in changing combinations. There are also special exhibitions dedicated to modern artists and tendencies.

Museum of Modern Art
Domstr. 10
60311 Frankfurt am Main
Phone 0 69/21 23 04 47
Fax 0 69/21 23 78 82
mmk@stadt-frankfurt.de
www.mmk-frankfurt.de

Business hours
Tue, Thu – Sun 10 am –
5 pm, Wed 10 am – 8 pm
Admission
€ 6.–, reduced € 3.–,
last Sat. in month
admission free

Museum of Modern Art

The street Braubachstraße with its art and antique shops and the **Museum of Comical Art/Caricatura**, which is accommodated in house number 30-34, leads to the Römerberg, which opens to the left into a wide square. The Römer, the historical town hall, faces the eastern row of half-timbered houses. To their left, there is the Stone House, the Steinerne Haus, which was originally built as a late Gothic patrician house in 1464. This is the home of the **Frankfurt Art Association, "Kunstverein"**. In changing exhibitions, the institution shows the recent work of individual artists as well as thematic group exhibitions.

The art gallery **Schirn Kunsthalle** lies between the eastern row of half-timbered houses and the cathedral. It is a location for extravagant exhibitions of international importance. In the past, some of the topics were: Modern Art in Vienna, Expressionism, Surrealism and Dadaism, Art and Consumption, Art

Frankfurt Art Association
Steinernes Haus
am Römerberg
Markt 44
60311 Frankfurt am Main
Phone 0 69/2 19 31 40
Fax 069/21 93 14 11

post@fkv.de
www.fkv.de
Business hours
Tue – Sun 11 am – 7 pm
Admission
€ 6.–, reduced € 4.–

Art gallery, Schirn-Kunsthalle

under Stalin, the painter association Nazarener, and Summer of Love. Extensive retrospectives were devoted to Marc Chagall, Wassily Kandinsky, Frida Kahlo, Henri Matisse, Yves Klein, James Ensor, Max Beckmann and other artists.

> **Schirn Art Gallery**
> **Frankfurt**
> Römerberg
> 60311 Frankfurt am Main
> Phone 0 69/2 99 88 20
> Fax 0 69/2 99 88 22 40
> welcome@schirn.de
>
> www.schirn.de
> Business hours
> Tue, Fri – Sun 10 am – 7 pm,
> Wed, Thu 10 am – 10 pm
> Admission
> variable, depends on exhibition

The **Struwwelpeter-Museum** is integrated within the building of the Schirn Art Gallery. "Struwwelpeter", (Shock-headed Peter), is a famous children's book written by the doctor and psychiatrist Dr. Heinrich Hoffmann (1809-1894). Apart from the original scripts and other picture books by the author, the museum presents many different editions from all over the world, as well as numerous parodies. Additionally, there are works by children and artists that show the "Struwwelpeter" today.

Struwwelpeter-Museum
Schirn, Römerberg,
Bendergasse 1
60311 Frankfurt am Main
Phone 0 69/28 13 33
Fax 0 69/55 45 77

www.struwwelpeter-museum.de
Business hours
Tue – Sun 11 am – 5 pm
Admission free

Return
O Underground U4, U5
   Stop Dom / Römer
   to Hauptbahnhof
   or 10 min walk to Hauptwache
   from there underground and S-Bahn to all directions

International bestseller:
Der Struwwelpeter (Shock-headed Peter)

Honouring the Saviour
Pilgrimage for true and non-believers to churches, monasteries and the cathedral

Once, the cathedral and the churches were rising up to the sky, determining life and townscape. Frankfurt's houses of God, although now towered above by the capitalistic cathedrals are witnesses of history.

Pilgrimage for true and non-believers to churches, monasteries and the cathedral

Church, Katharinenkirche;
Previous pages:
Cathedral, Kaiserdom
St. Bartholomäus

The walk, about two kilometres long, starts at Hauptwache, which is called the Heart of the Town. Underground and regional trains arrive here, coming from all directions.

Opposite the Hauptwache, there is the church **Katharinenkirche**, where Johann Wolfgang Goethe was confirmed and Friedrich Stoltze got married. The ingenious, modest baroque building had replaced the former medieval church of a hospital. It was built according to the plans of Melchior Heßler, from 1678 to 1681.

Behind the church Katharinenkirche, the street Holzgraben leads to the left towards Liebfrauenstraße and Liebfrauenberg. A chapel of the Virgin Mary had been situated on this site since around 1310. In 1344 it was modified, becoming a hall church. After several extensions, the Catholic church **Liebfrauenkirche** was renovated in late Gothic style in the 15th century. The church has survived the Reformation, and since 1917 it has been used as a monastery church by Capuchin monks.

The street Neue Kräme goes southwards, and after having crossed Berliner Straße, one can see the square Paulsplatz with its church **Paulskirche** to the right. A monastery of Franciscan friars had been located on this place since 1271, which was

replaced by a church of a mendicant order of the Catholic church in 1485. During the Reformation, in 1529, the monks handed the monastery and its church over to the town council, and it became the town's principal Protestant church. By 1782, the church was rather ramshackle and had to be pulled down. In 1787, the construction of the new church Paulskirche was started, and the classicistic church was finally finished in 1833. The church was also used by the delegates of the first all-German parliament, the National Assembly, in 1848. Nowadays, the church is a popular location for important events.

Following the course of the street Braubachstraße, one gets to the Römer, the historical town hall. At its south-eastern corner, the Limpurger Gasse turns right and gives way to the Münzgasse until the **monastery of the Carmelite monks**. These monks had fled from the mountain Karmel to Europe in order to escape from the turmoil of the crusades. They had been establishing a monastery in Frankfurt since

"Anbetung der Heiligen Drei Könige" (Worship of the Three Wise Men), painting by Jörg Ratgeb, around 1510

1246, which was renovated in late Gothic style between 1460 and 1520. In the cloisters of this monastery, the artist Jörg Ratgeb painted from 1514 to 1521 the largest mural to the north of the Alps. Parts of the painting, which is 140 metres long, showing the birth, life and death of Jesus Christ, have been conserved. On the walls of its refectory, Ratgeb painted the history of the Carmelites. Back in Southern Germany, the painter sided with the revolutionary farmers and helped organising their troops. In 1526, after the suppression of the farmers, Ratgeb was tortured and quartered on the market square in Pforzheim.

Today, the monastery is used by the Institute for City History. In different exhibitions, parts of the historical treasures can be seen there time and again, such as the "Golden Bull" from 1356, the most important law of the constitution of the German Reich until 1806.

Institute for City History **Carmelite Monastery** Münzgasse 9 60311 Frankfurt am Main Phone 0 69/21 23 79 14 Fax 0 69/21 24 44 39	michael.fleiter@stadt-frankfurt.de www.stadtgeschichte-ffm.de Business hours Mon – Fri 8.30 am – 5 pm, Sat, Sun 10 am – 5 pm Admission free

The church **Kirche St. Maria** belongs to the complex of the Carmelite monastery. It stems from the second half of the 13th century, and since 1424 it had been renovated in late Gothic

Frankfurt Museum of Archaeology Karmelitergasse 1 60311 Frankfurt am Main Phone 0 69/21 23 58 96 Fax 0 69/21 23 07 00 info.archaeolmus@stadt-frankfurt.de	www.archaeologisches-museum-frankfurt.de Business hours Tue – Sun 10 am – 5 pm, Wed 10 am – 8 pm Admission € 4.–, reduced € 2.–

style. Today, it is the location of the Frankfurt Museum of Archaeology. The church and its newly built annex present prehistoric, Roman, medieval and modern findings from Frankfurt and its surroundings, complemented by a collection of the Classical Antiquity and the Old Orient.

The street Karmelitergasse leads to the alley Alte Mainzer Gasse. The Catholic parish church **Pfarrkirche St. Leonhard** rises between the alley and the Untermainkai. It was built as a late Roman basilica in 1219 and consecrated to St. Mary and St. George. In 1323, the church received an arm relic of St. Leonhard. For this reason, it changed its patronage. Around 1425 and again around 1500 to 1520 several Gothic modifications and extensions were realised.

Both, Alte Mainzer Gasse and the street by the river, lead to the Römerberg and its Historical Museum. The chapel of the hall court, **Palastkapelle**, dates from the 12th century and forms the eastern border of this complex of new and historical buildings.

The Protestant church **Alte Nikolaikirche** stands next to the Historical Museum. When its construction was started in 1250, it was meant to replace the small chapel of the hall

Church, Alte Nikolaikirche

court, and became the new church of the court. After 1458 it was rebuilt and became a late Gothic hall church.

Behind the eastern row, one can already see the **cathedral**. An old document tells us that "this church was newly built by the illustrious King Ludwig in 852, and consecrated to the Saviour (Salvator), the Lord Jesus Christ and the Blessed Virgin Mary, the twelve holy apostles, the martyrs and confessors and holy virgins and all patron saints, by Hrabanus, the bishop of the church in Mainz." In the 13th century, the church possessed relics such as the cranium of the martyr St. Bartholomew. From this time, the house of God was called Catholic parish church St. Bartholomew, "Pfarrkirche St. Bartholomäus". Since 1235 it had been transformed into a Gothic hall church. The plans of Madern Gerthener, who was one of the architects of the cathedral, were important for its further construction. They remained valid even after his death in 1430/31.

In 1356, the emperor Charles IV. passed a Reich basic law deciding that Frankfurt would become the place where the German kings should be elected. This law, which was called "Goldene Bulle" (bulla aurea / Golden Bull) due to the golden seal that had been tagged to it, belongs to the trea-

Cathedral, Kaiserdom
St. Bartholomäus

sures of the Institute for City History in the Carmelite monastery. Accordingly, the electors met in the chapel of the cathedral, the so-called Wahlkapelle, to elect the king. From 1562 to 1792, the cathedral was also the coronation church of the German emperors. Since then, it has also been called Kaiserdom, which means emperors' cathedral.

The Cathedral Museum, "Dommuseum", is situated in the cloisters of the cathedral. It contains valuable liturgical equipment, reliquaries and liturgical vestments, as well as the findings from a grave of a girl from the time of the Franconian king Mero, which were discovered in the cathedral in the course of excavations in 1992.

Cathedral Museum
Dom St. Bartholomäus
Domplatz 1
60311 Frankfurt am Main
Phone 069/13 37 61 86
Fax 069/13 37 61 85
dommuseum-ffm@t-online.de
Business hours
Tue–Fri 10am–5pm, Sat, Sun and holidays 11am–5pm
Admission
€ 2.–, reduced € 1.–

From the cathedral, the alley Kannengießergasse leads to Fahrgasse, and after some steps, the street Dominikanergasse starts at the right. Here, near the former eastern border of the town, the influential Dominican Order built their **Dominican monastery** in Frankfurt, starting in 1233. It was dissolved in 1803, and its art treasures were taken to the Historical Museum and the Städel. Nowadays, the monastery belongs to the regional association of the Protestant Church, and it is used for seminars, lectures, performances and exhibitions.

Return
The Dominican monastery is not far from the Konstablerwache (only 300 metres), from there underground and regional trains leave into all directions, also to Hauptwache and Hauptbahnhof.

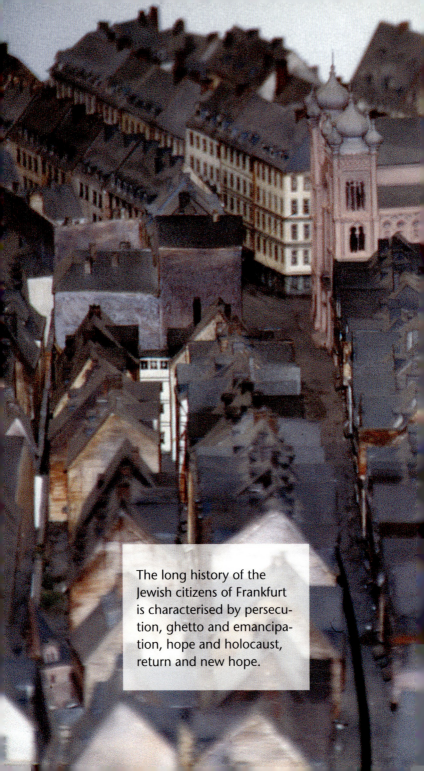

The long history of the Jewish citizens of Frankfurt is characterised by persecution, ghetto and emancipation, hope and holocaust, return and new hope.

The Despised Alley
The Rothschild family and the Jewish Frankfurt

The Rothschild family and the Jewish Frankfurt

Merchants, workmen and artists – since the 16th century often as religious refugees – from many different countries came to Frankfurt to naturalise. Already in the 9th century, Jews used to live in Frankfurt. The first Jewish parish was founded in the 12th century, and Christians and Jews lived together peacefully. Because of the forced christening of a Jewish boy in 1241, the first Jewish protests occurred and caused the first "Frankfurt Battle against the Jews". 180 Jews were killed, the remaining 24 people were baptised.

Since 1270, Jews settled down again in town. During the Plague epidemic, which had reached Frankfurt in 1349, more than 2000 people died. Flagellants from Würzburg came into town and blamed the Jews for the Plague. They caused a blood bath among the Jews and set fire to their houses. The flames spread to the town hall and the convent St. Bartholomew. At the beginning, the Frankfurt Christians supported their Jewish neighbours. But when the rumour was spread that the Jews had set fire to the church Bartholomäuskirche, they also participated in the prosecution of the Jews.

Walls of the Jewish ghetto,
Judengasse with synagogue in the Judengasse Museum

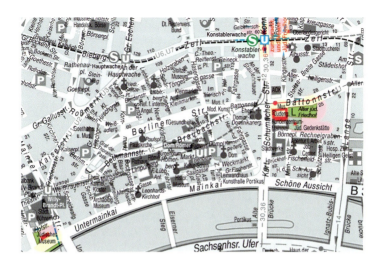

A new Jewish parish developed in Frankfurt in 1360. However, in 1458 the Jews were moved from the quarter around the cathedral to the other side of the eastern town wall. There, a Jewish ghetto, called **Judengasse,** was established, where people had to live and work crowdedly together.

In 1613, the journeymen rebelled against patrician mismanagement and corruption. The gingerbread baker Vinzenz Fettmilch, who was supported by the guilds and several merchants, made himself the leader of the movement and accused the Jews of being guilty, too. Their quarter, the Judengasse, was plundered in 1614, and their inhabitants were expelled from town. The rebellion was stopped by the emperor; Fettmilch and others were executed. And the Jews came back.

The 18th century was famous for its tolerance and the enlightenment, thus the

Chanukka-chandelier in the Jewish Museum

emancipation and assimilation of the Jews started. During the government of Charles of Dalberg, 1806 to 1813 under the supremacy of Napoleon, the Jews were given the same rights as the Christian Germans. After the French empire had been defeated, the German Alliance (Deutscher Bund) abolished equality in 1816. Only in 1864, the Jews received full civil rights in Frankfurt. The western row of the Judengasse was pulled down in 1872, the eastern row followed in 1882.

After 1811, the Jewish citizens of Frankfurt were no longer forced to live in the Judengasse, they became workers, craftsmen, bankers and factory owners, scientists and inventors, writers and artists, reactionary or revolutionary politicians, benefactors and founders for the town and their people – even as the other Germans did.

Due to the instigation of factory owners and big landowners, Adolf Hitler and his party Nationalsozialistische Deutsche Arbeiterpartei (NSDAP), the National Socialist German Labour Party, came into power on January 30, 1933 and anti-Semitism became a national doctrine. It was the beginning of the prosecution of political opponents and "Non-Aryans". The first concentration camps were established. Jewish

Jewish Museum, Rothschild-Palace

shops were boycotted. Many people, also Jewish people, participated in the resistance, or they fought against the Nazis in exile. Frankfurt, the town of industry, banks, trade and fairs, was reviled by the Nazis as "New-Jerusalem on the Franconian Jordan" and it was appointed to the "Town of the German Handicraft". On November 9, 1938, the synagogues in Frankfurt and in whole Germany were set on fire; this night of pogrom was named "Reichskristallnacht" by the Nazis. More and more Jews were deported to the camps, where they finally were killed.

In remembrance of the synagogue Börneplatz-Synagoge

Many of the approximately 30,000 Jews living in Frankfurt in 1933 emigrated. Family Frank with their daughter Anne, who wrote her diary in a Dutch hiding place, was one of them. After they had been revealed to the Nazis, Anne died in the concentration camp Bergen-Belsen in 1945. More than 10,000 Jews from Frankfurt were killed in concentration camps. At the end of the war, only 140 Jewish citizens had survived.

Meanwhile, there are again Jewish citizens living in town, the Jewish parish being part of the society and Frankfurt's community. Apart from the big synagogue Westendsynagoge, whose interior was devastated, although the building itself not destroyed, in 1938, there are other synagogues on the streets

Röderbergweg and Baumweg. At the same time, the youth centre Jugendbegegnungsstätte Anne Frank in Hansaallee 150 is offering a multimedia exhibition on the girl from Frankfurt. The Jewish community centre is a place that is dedicated to the present and the future. In the Jewish museum, history can be experienced.

The tram lines 11 and 12 and the underground lines U1 to U5 stop at the square Willy-Brandt-Platz with the municipal theatre, "Theater der Städtischen Bühnen". The street Neue Mainzer Straße passes the theatre and leads to Untermainkai. Just around the right hand corner one can see the palace Rothschild-Palais, which was built in 1820 and bought 1846 by Baron Mayer Carl von Rothschild. Banners are announcing the **Jewish Museum**.

The first part of the historical exhibition shows the development of the Jewish community from the beginning of their settlement in Germany and in Frankfurt until the dissolution of the ghetto on Judengasse. The second part of the historical exhibition aims at the time since 1800, and it also documents the prosecution and genocide by the Nazis. The section "Jewish life – Jewish celebrations" illustrates daily life, public holidays and celebrations. Cult objects demonstrate religious practice at home and in the synagogue. The history of the family and the bank Rothschild are presented in the smoking parlour, the Rauchsalon, of the palace. Art and other special exhibitions supplement the extensive permanent exhibition.

Jewish Museum Frankfurt	Business hours
Rothschild-Palais	Tue – Sun 10 am – 5 pm,
Untermainkai 14 – 15	Wed 10 am – 8 pm
60311 Frankfurt am Main	Admission
Phone 0 69/21 23 50 00	€ 2.60, reduced € 1.30
Fax 0 69/21 23 07 05	Combiticket Jewish
info@juedischesmuseum.de	Museum/Judengasse
www.juedischesmuseum.de	Museum € 3.–, reduced € 1.50

In remembrance of the killed Jews from Frankfurt

The Jewish Museum is about 1.5 kilometres away from the Museum Judengasse. A nice walk goes upstream, along the Main, passing historical buildings, which are towered above by the Frankfurt skyline. At the bridge Alte Brücke, the way turns left into Kurt-Schumacher-Straße. On the right-hand side Rechneigrabenstraße branches off and broadens to the square Neuer Börneplatz with the **memorial** to the killed Frankfurt Jews. Until 1938, this was the place of the synagogue, which was burnt down in the pogrom night on November 9. The stones were used for the main cemetery, and they still have the black traces of the fire.

Go from the memorial Börneplatz back to Kurt-Schumacher-Straße. The entrance to the **Museum Judengasse,** an annex of the Jewish Museum, is situated right at the corner Battonstraße. Here, you can see the foundations and walls of some houses of the Judengasse from the 15th to 18th century. These remains were found in the course of construction works. Together with pictures, documents and other exhibits, they tell us the story of the ghetto and its inhabitants.

"Mayer Amschel Rothschild bewahrt den Schatz des Kurfürsten, neben ihm seine Frau Gutle" (Mayer Amschel Rothschild keeps the treasure of the prince elector, next to him his wife Gutle), painting by Moritz Daniel Oppenheim, 1859

Family Rothschild belonged to them. Mayer Amschel Rothschild (1744-1812) founded a bank in 1766 and gave also shares to his five sons, who later became the directors of the banks in Frankfurt, London, Paris, Vienna and Naples. Gutle Rothschild, his wife and the mother of his five sons, stayed in the family's house in Frankfurt until her death.

The Danish teller of fairy tales Hans Christian Andersen writes: "… servants with burning candles in heavy, silver chandeliers were standing there, deeply bending before the old woman, who was carried downstairs in an armchair. The owner of the house stood bareheaded and respectfully kissed her hand. It was his mother. She friendly nodded to him and the servants, and they accompanied her through a narrow alley to a small house; it was her home, here, she had given birth to her children, and here all her happiness had blossomed, if she left the despised alley and the small house, she would not be happy any longer! That is what she believed…"

Rothschild's bank in Frankfurt was dissolved in 1901. In 1944, the Rothschild house was destroyed by bombs. As long as the Rothschild family lived in Frankfurt – until 1924 – they were benefactors of the town and their people.

Special exhibitions in the Museum Judengasse are dedicated to different topics. In the educational centre "Oskar und Emilie Schindler Lernzentrum", one can read the CVs of Frankfurt Jews who were deported and killed, their names being written on the walls of the memorial and the old Jewish cemetery.

Judengasse Museum
Kurt-Schumacher-Str. 10
60311 Frankfurt am Main
Phone 0 69/2 97 74 19
Fax 0 69/21 23 07 05
info@juedischesmuseum.de
www.judengasse.de
www.juedischesmuseum.de

Business hours
Tue – Sun 10 am – 5 pm,
Wed 10 am – 8 pm
Admission
€ 1.50, reduced € 0.70
Combiticket Jewish
Museum/Judengasse
Museum
€ 3.–, reduced € 1.50

The old **Jewish cemetery** stretches between the memorial and Battonstraße. You will get the key for the entrance Battonstraße at the counter of the Museum Judengasse. From the 12th century until 1828, this cemetery was used as a place of burial, and after the cemetery Heiliger Sand in Worms, it is the oldest Jewish cemetery in Germany. The oldest gravestone that is conserved dates from the year 1227.

Alter Jüdischer Friedhof,
Old Jewish cemetery

Great part of the cemetery is a lawn, which was also covered with graves in the past. The middle and the eastern burial ground have still remained. Some of the gravestones have fallen down or sunk into the ground. Jewish cemeteries are the property of the dead, and in their function as homes of eternity or houses of the future life until the end of time, they shall remain untouched. The cemetery was closed in 1828, and it remained untouched for more than 100 years. In 1943, the Nazis started destroying that cemetery, which also hides the modest gravestone of Meyer Amschel Rothschild.

Return
from Konstablerwache, which is about 300 metres away, regional or underground trains in all directions – or
Continuation from Konstablerwache
O U5 direction Preungesheim Stop Nibelungenallee/Deutsche Bibliothek

After the crossroads Nibelungenallee/Eckenheimer Landstraße, the street Rat-Beil-Straße turns left and after 500 metres, it arrives at the cemetery **Israelitischer Friedhof**, which was used as a burial place from 1828 to 1929. Except for Saturdays or Jewish holidays, the cemetery is open from 9 am to 6 pm. During a walk, one will discover the gravestones of the family Rothschild, Paul Ehrlich, Leopold Cassella, Moritz Daniel Oppenheim, Leopold Sonnemann and other Frankfurters.

Back to Eckenheimer Landstraße, along the main cemetery, the way leads after 500 metres to the entrance of the burial ground **Neuer Jüdischer Friedhof**, which is the New Jewish Cemetery. Except for the Sabbath, the cemetery is open everyday until 5 pm. The inner portal carries the epigraph: "I will promenade before the countenance of the Everlasting, in the realms of life." This promise is also valid for the 800 citizens of Frankfurt who escaped from murder and deportation by the Nazis between 1941 and 1942 by suicide.

Cemetery Israelitischer Friedhof

Return
O Underground U5
   Stop Hauptfriedhof
   to Konstablerwache and from there to Hauptbahnhof

Frankfurt has so many goods
Shopping in Frankfurt's city

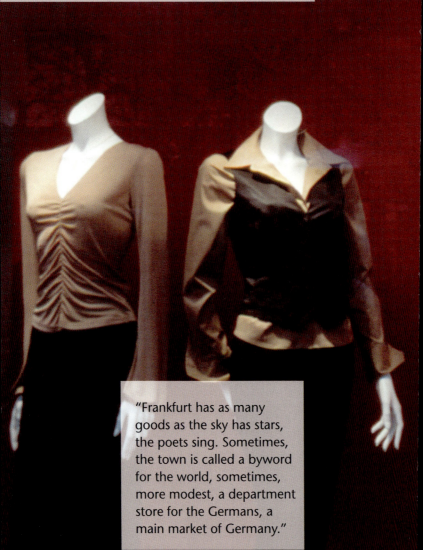

"Frankfurt has as many goods as the sky has stars, the poets sing. Sometimes, the town is called a byword for the world, sometimes, more modest, a department store for the Germans, a main market of Germany."

LOVE IS GIVING

Shopping in Frankfurt's city

The quotation we put at the beginning is still valid today. It is taken from "Ansichten von Frankfurt am Main" (Images of Frankfurt on the Main), a work published by the Frankfurt historian and theologian Anton Kirchner (1779-1835) in 1818.

There are plenty of shopping malls, shopping centres, department stores, farmers' markets and weekly markets in town. Many inhabitants of Frankfurt have their favourite streets, which are lined by shops of all kind, meeting all demands, from rather ordinary to luxury goods. And of course, numerous pubs, restaurants, snack bars and fast food restaurants take their place among the shops, allowing the strollers and shopaholics to have a rest and regain their strength. There are some streets that are worth mentioning, for example Berger Straße in Bornheim, Leipziger Straße in Bockenheim, Oeder Weg towards Nordend, Schweizer Straße in Sachsenhausen, and Schillerstraße from Hauptwache to Eschenheimer Turm.

All the others streets and squares around **Hauptwache** – Steinweg, Rathenauplatz and Goetheplatz, Rossmarkt, Kornmarkt, Liebfrauenberg, Töngesgasse, Neue Kräme, Berliner Straße – also invite you for strolling, watching and shopping.

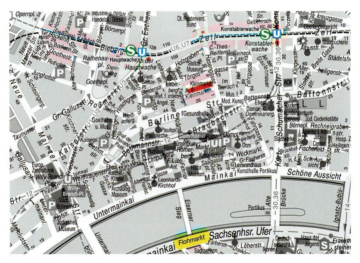

The Zeil, shopping mall

All over the world, the **Zeil**, in particular the 700 metre long pedestrian precinct from Hauptwache to Konstablerwache, is known as Germany's top-selling shopping mall. Here, you get everything your heart desires and your purse or credit card permits. It is also the place where you will find the big department stores, such as Galeria Kaufhof (Zeil 116-126) and Karstadt (Zeil 90), which consist of many floors and which sell everything, from dainties to toys, from fashion to media. Who wants to pay less, buys at Woolworth (Zeil 94).

Right next to Kaufhof, the shopping gallery **Zeilgalerie** (Zeil 112-114) is made up of more than 50 shops and restaurants on eight floors, offering fashion – Benetton, Empire, Essence, New Stylez – and watches, water pipes and Teddy & More. From the outlook platform on the top of the shopping gallery, one can look over Frankfurt and its exciting rising skyline, from 2008 on also on the new shopping centre "FrankfurtHoch4" with its skyscrapers near the Zeil.

There are many fashion shops of all kinds on the Zeil, small and big ones, shops that are offering clothes at low and high prices, as well as luxury shops. To all these shops belong, among others: Esprit (Zeil 121), Mexx (119), New Yorker (107), Hennes & Mauritz (85-93), Zara (72-82), Eckerle (79), Peek & Cloppenburg (71-75), C & A (48). Some specialist shops are also situated in between, for example the watch-maker's shop Pletsch (81), or Leder-Gabler (69) for leather goods, as well as perfume shops like Kobberger (127) and Douglas (100). And behind the church Katharinenkirche, where the Zeil starts with high numbers, the jeweller Lueg has his fine shop.

The square Konstablerwache extends at the other end of the pedestrian precinct. In the past, this was the place of a guard house similar to the police station Hauptwache, and it is also an underground station where regional and underground trains stop. The square is used for various events, and two days a week, Thursday between 10 am and 8 pm and Saturday between 8 am and 5 pm, more than 50 stalls offer mainly local products. On this market, called **Erzeugermarkt Konstablerwache**, one can buy fresh fruits and vegetables, meat, sausages and fish, bread, rolls and cake, but one might also have a chat or take a small snack – the rich supply reaches from Kartoffelpuffer mit Apfelmus (potato fritters with apple purée) to local specialities, such as Fleischwurst, Grie Soß and Frankfurt's famous cider, Ebbelwei.

Zeil-Information
www.zeil-online.de
www.zeilgalerie.de
www.erzeugermarkt-konstablerwache.de

On the way back from Konstablerwache to Hauptwache, the alley Hasengasse leads down to the left. After 200 metres, one has reached a unique gourmet temple: the **market hall Kleinmarkthalle**. It is a paradise for gourmets, consisting of 90 shops and stalls. Fruits and vegetables, herbs and spices, sausages, meat, game, poultry and fish, bread, cakes and pastries, dairy products and flowers are spread out before the eyes of the buyer

In Kleinmarkthalle, market hall

in tempting variety. The alluring supply does not only come from Frankfurt and its surroundings. Food and semi-luxury come from all over the world. The Kleinmarkthalle, which was originally opened in 1879 and newly built after the war, in 1954, is called "a hearty piece of Frankfurt".

From the other entry and exit of the market hall at Liebfrauenberg the street Liebfrauenstraße is leading back to Hauptwache.

Kleinmarkthalle
Hasengasse 5 – 7
60311 Frankfurt am Main
www.kleinmarkthalle.de

Business hours
Mo – Fri 7.30 am – 6 pm,
Sat 7.30 am – 3 pm

Hauptwache is also the starting point for the walk through Kalbächer Gasse and the following street Große Bockenheimer Straße, which together carry the name **Fressgass**, which means stuffing alley. In the northwestern corner of the square An der Hauptwache, the place where the Struwwelpeter-fountain is bubbling, Biebergasse leads via Rathenauplatz to the Fressgass, which stretches about 500 metres to the opera Alte Oper. This street, which is a pedestrian precinct, has more to offer than only cafés and restaurants. Already the delicatessen Zarges on Kalbächer Gasse 10 and Plöger on Große Bockenheimer Straße 30 justify its nickname.

Plöger Delikatessen, delicatessen

On Fressgass, you can buy fashion at Akris (Große Bockenheimer Straße 13), tempting lingerie at Valentina (52), shoes at Timberland Store (19), Mark (7) and Petra Dieler (35). Eterna Excellent (25) and Milano (30) offer a great choice of ties and other accessoires for men and gentlemen. Georg Ewald runs a second-hand bookshop (29), the gallery Arizona-Galerie (37) offers American Indian jewellery and Swarovski (8) flamboyant fashion design.

Small choice of the immense dainties of Plöger Delikatessen. Prepared for you by our chefs in masterly fashion.

Just to the left of the crossroads Fressgass and Neue Mainzer Straße, **Goethestraße** is leading back to Rathenauplatz and Hauptwache. On the other side of Neue Mainzer Straße, the opera Alte Oper on the square Opernplatz rises in all its splendour. The last 300 metres on Goethestraße prove that Frankfurt is not lagging behind Paris or Madrid, London or New York in terms of shopping.

There is, for example, fashion by Burberry (Goethestraße 34), Ermangildo Zegna (31-33), Möller & Schaar (26-28), Gucci (27), Hermès (25), Da Franca (23), Versace (22), Bogner (21), Pfüller (15-17), Louis Vuitton (13), Chanel (10), Hugo Boss (3), Salvatore Ferragamo (2), children's fashion by Pfüller (12), men's fashion by Uli Knecht (35), and Armani (19). Earlston (4-8) is a bespoke tailor for men.

Those walking through Frankfurt need good shoes. You can buy good and exclusive shoes in Goethestraße at Valleverde (37), Tod's (31-33), Linda (26-28), Camper (18), Fink Exclusiv (9), bags at Picard Galerie (14) and at Aigner Shop (4-8), where

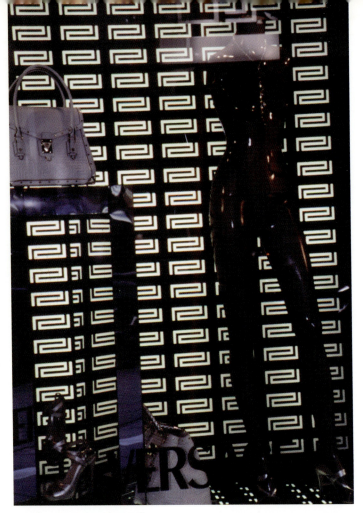

On the street Goethestraße

you can also get fashion and accessoires. Glasses that are real pieces of jewellery are sold by Rainer Brenner (24), watches are sold at the watchmaker's shop Glashütte. And, of course, Goethestraße is the location of jewellery designers like Ehinger-Schwarz (18), Michèle M. (4) and the world-famous jewellers Tiffany (20), Bulgari (16), Cartier (11), Wempe (10) and Friedrich (9). Artistic jewellery made of china, objects by famous artists, and also crockery, designed and ornamented by artists, are for sale in the Rosenthal –Studio (1). And who ever does not want to sign his postcard from Frankfurt with a ball-point, calls at the shop Montblanc Boutique (29).

Goethestraße-Information
www. goethestrasse-frankfurt.de

The **flea market** on the southern bank of the Main, the Museums' Bank, is a popular destination for people from Frankfurt and its surroundings. Coming by underground, lines U4 and U5, you have to get off the train at the station Dom/Römer. The walk of about 600 metres takes you over Römerberg to the Main, over the footbridge Eiserner Steg, and finally to the other side of the river. From there until the next footbridge, which is a distance of about one kilometre, stalls are lining up in endless rows – every Saturday between 9 am and 2 pm.

Real fine art and real trash, that is what you will find on the flea market; odds and ends, antiquities, jewellery, old and new books, comics, records and discs, videos and DVDs, furniture, first and second hand household articles, toys, tools and clothing from hat to shoe.

Return
O   Underground U4, U5
    Stop Dom/Römer

On the flee market

The philosopher and politician of education Wilhelm von Humboldt, who loved staying in Frankfurt, spoke about the "beautifully arranged plantations" in 1828.

Beautifully arranged plantations
The Plantation Ring, the Senckenberg Museum of Natural History, Palm Garden and Zoo

The Plantation Ring, the Senckenberg Museum, Palm Garden and Zoo

Once, the ramparts, consisting of earthwalls, walls, bulwarks and ditches, surrounded the old Frankfurt, protecting it against enemies. However, in modern times, these constructions had lost their purpose and hindered the extension of the town. For this reason, the council decided to pull down the fortifications in 1805. From 1806 to 1813, during Napoleon's supremacy, Frankfurt was governed by Karl von Dalberg, archbishop and prince elector of Mainz. Maire Guiollet, commissioner of the building authority in Frankfurt, let rapidly demolish the ramparts. The town gardener Sebastian Rinz planted parks and gardens, which until today have been equipped with so many fountains, sculptures and monuments, that it is impossible to mention all of them.

Over a distance of about four kilometres, the **plantation ring** is surrounding the city. By walking along, one experiences nature and culture, one sees a fair bit of sights and passes many skyscrapers. Such a walk could, for example, start with the plan-

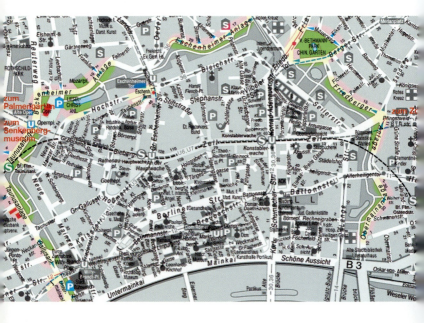

Monument to Friedrich Schiller;
Previous pages: Monument to Ludwig van Beethoven

tations on the lower Main, Untermainanlage, at Schauspielhaus on the square Willy-Brandt-Platz. You get there by tram, lines 11 and 12, or underground, lines U1 to U5.

Since 1910, the **Untermainanlage** has been embellished by the Märchenbrunnen, the Fairy Tale Fountain. A washergirl from Frankfurt was the model for the snow-white beauty. The sculpture that stands on the plantation **Gallusanlage** is unmistakably Goethe. In the past, the monument from 1840 was situated on the square Goetheplatz, where it will return again soon.

Schiller, whose monument from 1864 had originally been erected at Hauptwache, is now waiting on the plantation

Taunusanlage. Further to the right, one sees Snow White, a sculpture that stems from the 50s. To the left, the monument of Heinrich Heine, created by the sculptor Georg Kolbe in 1913. His Beethoven monument was set up on a hill in 1948. The composer is a heroic and erotic male figure accompanied by two beauties, the thinking and the calling beauty.

To the left of the main path, Eduardo Chilida erected his concrete sculpture "Ein Haus für Goethe" (A House for Goethe) in 1986. There are other sculptures on both sides of the path, among them "Flora", "Liegende" (The Reclining) and "Aufforderung" (Invitation to dance). The Guiolett monument from 1837 lies to the left. In the middle of the plantation, there is the Marshall fountain in honour of the American Secretary of State who had started the Western German economic miracle after the Second World War by his so-called Marshall plan. The fountain with its three Graces of bronze was designed by Toni Stadler in 1963.

Before the eyes of the stroller, the opera **Alte Oper** rises in all its splendour and all its architectural and sculptural pomp. The

Alte Oper, opera

In the Palm Garden

nice Lucae fountain, which is bubbling on the square in front of the opera, reminds us of the architect Richard Lucae, whose plans were used for the construction of the opera between 1873 and 1880. In 1944, the opera was destroyed by bombs. After its reconstruction in 1981, the opera has again been a location for concerts, opera balls and other performances.

Bockenheimer Landstraße also starts at the Opernplatz. Those who want to interrupt their strolls over the plantation ring, which might be divided into several stages, now walk along Bockenheimer Landstraße. Historical Westend houses as well as modern office buildings are lining that street. After one kilometre, Palmengartenstraße lies at the right hand side and leads you after a few steps to the **Palm Garden**.

If you want to explore the Palm Garden in all its variety, you will need several hours, going on a travel through the botany all over the world. Here, all kinds of plants are growing and flourishing – huge palm trees, multicoloured orchids, water lilies and pansies, as well as bizarre plants from the earth's dry zones.

In 1869, the garden architect Heinrich Siesmayer created a nature park for the citizens of the town. By then, the palm house, which is the core of the plantation, was home for plants from inaccessibly far regions. Since then, the Palm Garden has been growing steadily, and now it also accommodates, apart from historical buildings, modern green house complexes, which show the plant world in its breathtaking wealth. 19,000 square metres out of the area of 22 hectares are covered by glass. The attractive park integrates different thematic gardens as well as leisure facilities for young and old. Children take the palm express or they paddle on the pond. Changing flower and informational exhibitions and an extensive cultural programme make the visit a great experience in every season.

Palm Garden
Palmengartenstr. 11
Siesmayerstr. 63
60323 Frankfurt am Main
Phone 0 69/21 23 66 89,
21 23 39 39
Fax 0 69/21 23 78 56
info.palmengarten@stadt-frankfurt.de

www.palmengarten-frankfurt.de
Business hours
daily Nov – Jan 9 am – 4 pm,
Feb – Oct 9 am – 6 pm
Admission
€ 6.–, reduced € 3.–

Following Bockenheimer Landstraße for about 200 metres, one will get to the square at **Bockenheimer Warte**. This late Gothic watch-tower from 1435 was part of the defences that surrounded the town at far distance. At the square, the plantation Senckenberganlage turns left and reaches the Senckenberg Museum of Natural History after another 300 metres.

Jurassic Park on the Main, that is how people call the museum, for skeletons and models of dinosaurs belong to its attractions. It illustrates the origin and development of the earth and life in general, until the genesis of the human being. There are also some fossils from the pit Messel near Darmstadt, where the famous primeval horse was discovered. Dioramas show animals in their habitats, and the underwater world allows its visitors to experience the variety of sea life and freshwater fish. One of the larger departments of the museum is dedicated to the mummies of the Ancient Egypt.

Senckenberg Museum of Natural History
Senckenberganlage 25
60325 Frankfurt am Main
Phone 0 69/7 54 20
Fax 0 69/74 62 38
www.senckenberg.de

Business hours
Mon, Tue, Thu, Fri 9 am – 5 pm, Wed 9 am – 8 pm, Sat, Sun, holidays 9 am – 6 pm
Admission
€ 6.–, reduced € 3.–

Return
Stop Bockenheimer Warte
O Underground U4 to Hauptbahnhof
O Underground U6, U7 to Alte Oper and continue until Hauptwache

"Brachiosaurier" (Brachiosaurian), painting by Klaus Dill, 1994, with the help of the Senckenberg Museum of Natural History

The next part of our walk through the **Plantation Ring**, "Anlagenring", starts at the opera Alte Oper. Behind the building, the **Bockenheimer Anlage** leads to the right. In the Second World War, the water of the pond was used by the fire brigade to extinguish fire. With its name Liesel-Christ-Anlage, the park commemorates the great folk actress and theatre director. One of the sculptures, "Torso II", was created by Waldemar Grzimek in 1973. The classicistic garden house "Nebbiensches Gartenhaus" from 1810 is situated only some steps farther. Today, it is used for exhibitions, concerts and other events. To the right side of the plantation, a commemorative plaque is devoted to the writer Ludwig Börne.

Between Bockenheimer and Eschenheimer Anlage the late Gothic tower **Eschenheimer Turm** rises. It was completed as part of the defence by the architect of the cathedral, Madern Gerthener, from 1426 to 1428. When the fortifications were destroyed, the nice tower was spared.

On the plantation **Eschenheimer Anlage**, the inventor of the telephone, Philipp Reis, got his own monument, too. He had introduced his phone in Frankfurt in 1861. Furthermore, this is the place of the sculpture of the liberal priest and historian Anton Kirchner (1779 to 1835).

The Hessian monument, "Hessen-Denk-

Tower, Eschenheimer Turm

mal", which was cast from French canons, can be found on Friedberger Landstraße. It reminds us that Frankfurt was taken by the French army in 1792 and, in the same year, freed by Hessian and Prussian troops. The street Friedberger Landstraße leads over to **Friedberger Anlage**. The Bethmann park was designed as a Chinese garden. On the occasion of the 100th birthday of the banker Simon Moritz von Bethmann, his monument and not far away the "Odeon", the family's museum of sculptures from 1815, were set up here. In this part of the Plantation Ring, one finds the monument of the town gardener Sebastian Rinz, too, who had turned the former ramparts into gardens at the beginning of the 19th century.

Near the clock tower **Uhrtürmchen** from the year 1894, we are crossing the eastern end of the Zeil. Following Pfingstweidstraße to the left for about 300 metres, we will get to the zoo.

When, in 1858, the **Frankfurt Zoo** was founded, it was the second zoo in Germany. Professor Bernhard Grzimek, who was the director of the zoo from 1945 to 1974, became well-known as an ambassador for animals trough his film "Serengeti darf nicht sterben" (Serengeti must not die), his TV shows and many books. The zebra-striped plane he used for his Africa travels is to be seen in the zoo, too. More than 5,000 animals live in nearly actual environments,

and they feel good. A special experience is the visit at the Exotarium, where you can observe animals in their original environments – from the Antarctic of the penguins to the jungle of the crocodiles. In one part of the big aviary, birds can freely fly around, whereas in the Grzimek House day becomes night, which allows you to observe nocturnal animals and their behaviour. And of course, there is a petting zoo for the children.

Zoo Frankfurt Alfred-Brehm-Platz 16 60315 Frankfurt am Main Phone 0 69/21 23 37 35 Fax 0 69/21 23 78 55 info.zoo@stadt-frankfurt.de www.zoo-frankfurt.de	Business hours summertime daily 9 am – 7 pm, wintertime daily 9 am – 5 pm Admission € 7.–, reduced € 3.–, family ticket € 16.–, Saturday Special (last Sat in the month) € 5.–, children € 2.–

Return
O Underground U6, U7
   Stop Zoo
   to Hauptwache

In order to walk on the last part of the Plantation Ring, you should go back to the clock tower Uhrtürmchen, where you must now turn to the left. At Allerheiligentor – only the name of that street reminds us that this is the site of the former town gate – the plantation on the upper Main, **Obermainanlage**, starts. In the past, the monument of the poet Gotthold Ephraim Lessing was situated in front of the municipal library, which today is called Literaturhaus, the House of Literature. Close to the pond Rechneigraben-Weiher, which has remained of the former ditch

Monument to Gotthold Ephraim Lessing

of the town's fortification, one sees the grave of Maire Guiollet, who let pull down the defences in 1810. On the last part of the plantation, the philosopher Arthur Schopenhauer has also got his monument. At the House of Literature, the plantation ring finally meets the banks of the Main.

Return
O Tram 14
   Stop Hospital zum Heiligen Geist
   to Ostendstraße, change to
O S-Bahn S1-S6, S8, S9
   to Hauptwache or Hauptbahnhof

Behind Frankfurt the sea
Accompanying Robert Gernhardt through Frankfurt's Green Belt

The famous painter, drawer and poet Robert Gernhardt discovered and drew the Green Belt animal on one of his walks. This animal is the logo of the Green Belt that is surrounding Frankfurt.

Accompanying Robert Gernhardt through Frankfurt's Green Belt

Robert Gernhardt is a representative of the New Frankfurt School, "Neue Frankfurter Schule". Its drawers, painters and poets – F. K. Waechter, Chlodwig Poth, Hans Traxler, Bernd Pfarr and others – were concerned with enlightening and discerning reasoning, similar to the philosophers of the Frankfurt School, "Frankfurter Schule", around Theodor W. Adorno and Max Horkheimer, though by means of jokes, satire, irony, mockery and deeper sense.

It was a nice day in April 2002, when Robert Gernhardt discovered and drew the Green Belt animal. He confirmed that this creature was as seldom as a cross-breed of pig, newt and starling. The Umweltamt Frankfurt, the town's office for environmental care, sells the Green Belt animal in form of pins and toys, donating the profit to children's and youth projects in the Green Belt. For a small fee, the office also hands out a map indicating all nature walks around Frankfurt, all car parks and all stops of public transport, the "GrünGürtel Freizeitkarte".

GrünGürtel-Tier, the Green Belt animal discovered by Robert Gernhardt at Wörthspitze;
Previous pages: The bridge Niddabrücke leads to Wörthspitze in Höchst.

GrünGürtel Frankfurt
Umweltamt Frankfurt
Galvanistr. 28
60486 Frankfurt am Main
Phone 0 69/21 23 91 00
Fax 0 69/21 23 91 40

umwelttelefon@stadt-frankfurt.de
www.umweltamt.stadt-frankfurt.de
www.gruenguertel.de

About 8,000 hectare (which means 80,000,000 square metres), a third of the town's area, are meadows, fields, parks with playgrounds and leisure facilities, gardens, pastures and forests. These varied landscapes of the Green Belt, which are at the same time part of the regional park RheinMain, are the habitat of numerous kinds of plants and animals. Many paths and ways for strollers, hikers, bikers and riders lead through this nature reserve.

The symbol of the GrünGürtel-Rundwanderweg, which is a circular walk through the Green Belt, is a yellow dot with a blue and green semicircle. The belt is 63 kilometres long and it connects 70 sights and places of adventure. On the way, there are restaurants, places for a rest, shelters, camping sites, indoor and outdoor swimming pools and meadows for dogs. The Green Belt can be reached at several points by tram, underground and regional trains.

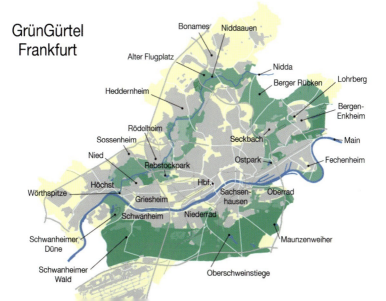

GrünGürtel Frankfurt

Spring time at the hill
Berger Hang

The Berger Rücken extends between Bad Vilbel and the northeastern Frankfurt districts **Seckbach** and **Bergen-Enkheim**. The vantage point Berger Warte is placed on its hill, to the left of the street Vilberer Landstraße, whereas the old Jewish cemetery, "Alter Jüdischer Friedhof", is situated to the right.

Arrival:
O Underground U7
from Hauptwache to terminus Enkheim, continue by
O Bus 940
to stop Berger Warte

Brunnenweg and Quellweg go from Bergen down to the southern slope of the hill. Passing the ornithological observation point and the fruit trail, one gets to the Enkheimer Ried and the forest Enkheimer Wald with its lake and its nature trail. The way leads along **Fechenheim** until "Bornheimer Hang", which borders the district **Bornheim** in the east. At the ice-rink near the Ostpark, this walk of about 10 kilometres can be finished.

Return
and arrival for the next part
O Underground U7
Stop Eissporthalle/Festplatz to or from Hauptwache

From the Ostpark, the walk around the Green Belt continues on Hanauer Landstraße, crosses the Main over the bridge Deutschherrnbrücke and arrives at the southern bank of the

Autumn at the pond Maunzenweiher

river. The tanner's mill in which Goethe used to stay, "Gerbermühle", is situated at the left, in direction to Offenbach. Today, the mill is a hotel and restaurant and a popular destination of excursions.

Through the vegetable gardens and the district of **Oberrad** the walk is now crossing the town's forest, Frankfurter Stadtwald. Starting at the pond Maunzenweiher, it climbs up to Oberschweinstiege at the big pond Jacobiweiher. Here, above **Sachsenhausen**, this part of the hike, which is about 11 kilometres long, can be terminated.

Return
and arrival for the next part
O Tram line 14
    Stop Oberschweinstiege to Südbahnhof, change to
O Underground U1, U2, U3 to Hauptwache or
O S-Bahn S5, S6 to Hauptbahnhof

From Oberschweinstiege the walk turns west, through the rich flora and fauna of the town's forest, passes **Niederrad** and **Schwanhcim**, where it finally crosses the major road B 40 in northern direction.

Those who are satisfied with the 13 kilometres through the forest can turn right on Schwanheimer Bahnstraße, and will get to the Kobelt-Zoo, which is open from May to September every Saturday between 2 pm and 7 pm, and on Sunday from 9 am to 7 pm. Afterwards, you will reach the historical station Schwanheim on Rheinlandstraße, which is the terminus of the former forest train, which took day tripper from Frankfurt's city to the country. Here, at the terminus, the traffic museum is installed and can be visited every Saturday, Sunday and on holidays from 10 am to 6 pm.

Return
and arrival for the next part
O Tram line 12, 19
    Stop Rheinlandstraße to Niederrad Bahnhof, change to
O S-Bahn S8, S9 to Hauptbahnhof or Hauptwache

From the station, the way leads westwards, either to Römerweg and the historical hiking trail to the bridge over the major road B 40, or to the nature trail Schwanheimer Wiesen, which starts at the forest playground.

If you take the bridge, just follow the symbol of the Green Belt, through the Schwanheimer Unterfeld, turn right at Kelsterbacher Weg, which leads you into the wood. Soon, the planking path through the great dune will start. You should not leave the path, otherwise you would endanger the sensitive vegetation of the dune.

10,000 years ago, after the last ice age, the wind deposited the sand from the river bed of the Main. A forest was growing

The dune at Schwanheim

Höchst, the tower of the castle and the church Justinuskirche

on the dune Schwanheimer Düne, which was partly cleared in the 19th century. Plum and cherry trees were planted instead. When a drought broke out in 1882, the trees became stunted and the sand reappeared. The dune moved, and in 1890 it arrived at its present place. As one of the few inland dunes in Europe (the closest can be found in Poland), the Schwanheimer Düne, which extends over 48 hectare, is particularly protected by nature conservation. Part of it is covered with the very seldom sweet grass bed, consisting of grey-hair grass, shepherd's grass, common thrift. Wild Orchids are growing on the meagre sand ground, pines and single cherry trees can be seen. In the past, the sand was cleared away. For this reason, the walk passes large fishing ponds. Straight on, we get to the Main, if we turn to the left afterwards, we will arrive at the ferry that takes hikers to Höchst. The Gernhardt ash trees that grow on the headland Wörthspitze at the mouth of the river Nidda, can be reached over a footbridge. They frame a stele showing the Green Belt animal. Here is the place where Robert Gernhardt saw and drew this funny creature.

The way from Schwanheim to this place is about 5 kilometres long. However, you must not miss a stroll through **Höchst**, a town, which in the past belonged to the electorate Mainz, becoming a district of Frankfurt in 1928. You will see its sights on the walk of about 2 kilometres through the alleys of the old centre.

The baroque palace Borongaropalast above the confluence of Nidda and Main was built from 1772 on for the Italian tobacco manufacturer Bolongaro, who had been denied the citizenship of Frankfurt. At the landing stage of the ferry, one sees the church Justinuskirche, one of the oldest churches in Germany. Its construction was already started in 790. Only a few steps take you from the square Justinusplatz to the square of the castle, the Schlossplatz, with its half-timbered houses. The castle with its high tower is a Renaissance building that was erected on the walls of another castle, a successor of an old Roman fortress that had been burned down by the people of Frankfurt in 1397. Nowadays, the castle includes a museum about Höchst and its history, which is open from Wednesday to Sunday between 10 am and 4 pm. On the Schlossplatz, the customs tower from the 14th century and the gate Maintor, which is about 100 years younger, remind us of the former fortifications of the town.

The castle, Höchster Schloss

Höchst's china is also sold at Kornmarkt, Berliner Straße 60

Höchst has gained importance due to the seat of the former company Hoechst AG. The china factory in Hoechst is older than the chemical industry. Founded in 1746, it was the third china factory in the Holy Roman Empire of the German Nations after Meißen and Vienna. Two merchants from Frankfurt and a porcelain painter who had fled from Meißen were awarded the privilege to produce china by the prince elector and archbishop of Mainz.

The street Bolongarostraße is only a few steps away from the Schlossplatz. The Porcelain Museum, which belongs to the Historical Museum Frankfurt, has its seat in the Kronberger House, a house of the aristocracy from the 16th century. More than 1,500 pieces of Höchster china can be marvelled at. In order to learn more about the porcelain and its production, you can additionally visit the Porcelain Manufactory, where you might also buy something, or see one of the special exhibitions. It is situated in Palleskestraße, which can be reached via Bolongarostraße until Zuckschwerdtstraße; turn left underneath the railway bridge and take the second street to the right.

Those who want to finish this part of the walk around the Green Belt, can go back from here by tram or from the station by S-Bahn.

Höchst Porcelain Museum
Kronberger Haus
Bolongarostr. 152
65929 Frankfurt-Höchst
Phone 0 69/21 24 54 74
Fax 0 69/21 23 07 02
info@historisches-museum.frankfurt.de

www.historisches-museum.frankfurt.de
Business hours
Sat, Sun, holidays
11 am – 6 pm
Admission
€ 2.50, reduced € 1.20

Höchst Porcelain Manufactory
Palleskestr. 32
65929 Frankfurt-Höchst
Phone 0 69/3 00 90 20
Fax 0 69/30 09 02 24
info@hoechster-porzellan.de

www.hoechster-porzellan.de
Business hours
Mon – Fri 9.30 am – 6 pm,
Sat 9.30 am – 2 pm
Admission
€ 5.–, reduced € 2.50

**Return
and arrival** for the next part
O Tram line 11
   Stop Zuckschwerdtstraße to Hauptbahnhof or Römer/Paulskirche
O S-Bahn S1, S2
   Stop Höchst to Hauptbahnhof or Hauptwache

The next part swings back and forth from the left to the right side of the river Nidda, going in northeastern direction – from Wörthspitze with the Gernhardt ash trees in Höchst, passing **Nied** and **Griesheim**, which are situated in the south, as well as **Sossenheim** in the north. If you take the subway underneath the motorway at Westkreuz Frankfurt and then follow the marked cycle track, you will get to the street Am Römerhof and the park Rebstockpark with the Frankfurt Narrow Gauge Railway Museum, the Frankfurt Feldbahnmuseum.

The Narrow Gauge Railway in the park Rebstockpark

Back on the bank of the river Nidda, the walk leads you through the parks Solmspark and Brentanopark, between **Rödelheim** to the left and **Bockenheim** to the right, afterwards along **Hausen** to the right and **Praunheim** to the left. Near **Ginnheim** on the right side the park Volkspark Niddatal and the forest Ginnheimer Wäldchen invite you for a short visit.

Frankfurt Narrow Gauge Railway Museum Am Römerhof 15a 60486 Frankfurt am Main Phone 0 69/70 92 92 ffmev@feldbahn-ffm.de www.feldbahn-ffm.de	Business hours first Fri of every month 5 pm – 7 pm without, first Sun of every month 2 pm – 5 pm with train tours Admission includes fare € 4.–, reduced € 2.–

Since the year 75, the borough **Heddernheim** was a Roman garrison and later, until the 3rd century, the political, economic and religious centre of an extensive Roman administrational district. By then, the town Nida had a port on the river Nidda. The findings from this "German Pompeji" are shown in the Archaeological Museum Frankfurt. In Heddernheim, there are hardly any traces left of the former Nida.

If you want to finish this stage of about 11 kilometres in Heddernheim, follow the street to the left of the bridge and after a few steps, you will get to the underground station.

**Return
and arrival** for the next part
O   Underground U1, U2, U3
     to Hauptwache

The last part of the walk around the Green Belt is supposed to start at Heddernheim. **Eschersheim** is extending to the right. Our way is winding eastwards through the pastures of the Nidda passing **Kalbach**, **Bonames** and **Harheim** on the left. On

Grape harvest at Lohrberg

the right-hand side near **Berkersheim**, the walk is leading away from the river, first turning south, then east, all along Bad Vilbel. Afterwards, the walk turns right again, all around Heiligenstock, where there is a nice view down on Frankfurt. Later, we follow the Eselsweg to Lohrberg, which is part of the mountain Berger Rücken, close to **Seckbach**.

The hill Lohrberg is about 180 metres high and is a vineyards of Frankfurt. The Riesling grapes yield approximately 8,000 to 9,000 bottles of wine and sparkling wine. In the pub Lohrberg-Schänke, you can try the wine immediately. Apart from that, there is the Beratungsgarten Lohrberg right at the slope of the hill, a garden where more than 500 different kinds of fruits are growing. Here, you do not only get information, but also complex guided tours for groups, associations, kindergartens, and school classes, as well as practical courses for hobby gardeners.

Information Garden Lohrberg
Klingenweg 90
60389 Frankfurt am Main

Phone 0 69/47 99 94
info@pvfrm.de
www.pvfrm.de

From Lohrberg, the walk all around the Green Belt continues in eastern direction and goes to Bergen-Enkheim. Those who have completed the last part of about 13 kilometres out of the total distance of 63 kilometres, have finally surrounded Frankfurt. The street Klingenweg at the Information Garden takes you south and after 300 metres you will reach Wilhelmshöher Straße, where the next bus stop is located.

Return
O Bus 43
   Stop Budge-Altenheim to Seckbacher Landstraße, change to
O Underground U4
   to Konstablerwache or Hauptbahnhof

Sex & crime in the city
The girl Rosemarie takes you through the night

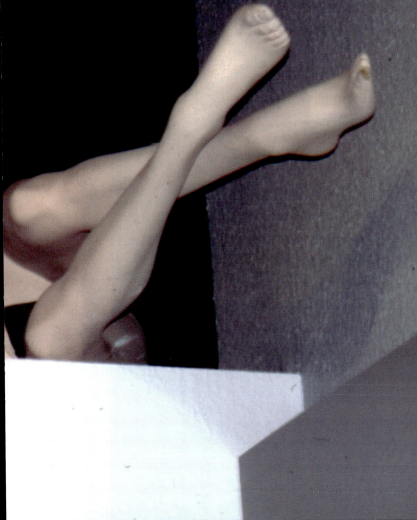

Two world-famous women from Frankfurt symbolise the disastrous connection between sex and crime: Rosemarie and Gretchen. But there is also crime without sex and sex without manslaughter and murder.

The girl Rosemarie takes you through the night

Frankfurt is often disparaged as a stronghold of crime. Frankfurt's enemies like quoting figures, in order to prove that the town resembles Chicago – invoking the past times of Al Capone.

Every passport offence, every single deal with drugs enter the statistics. Due to the fact that Frankfurt's airport is the central airport of Europe, these offences numerously appear in the figures of the criminal pedants.

The chance to be killed in Frankfurt is far smaller than it is in our capital Berlin or Handel's Halle or in the Hanseatic Bremen. Also in terms of robbery, burglary, car theft and other crimes, Frankfurt lies far behind other German cities. In cities like Hannover, Magdeburg and many other towns, one should worry more about his property. Also when talking about sexual acts of violence, Frankfurt is not at the top. The Catholic Cologne, for example, comes far ahead of Frankfurt. Frankfurt is also Bankfurt, which means that the town has a lot of business crimes, the bourse and banks being the scene of the crimes, managers being the perpetrators.

For some people, prostitution might be a sin. However, the granting and fulfilment of lust is

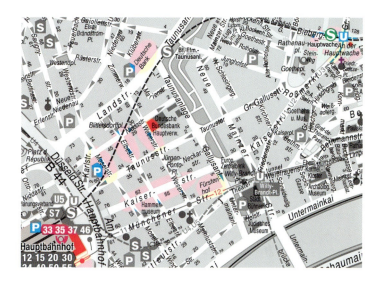

not criminal. The women, who proudly call themselves "Huren", bitches, are sexual workers who meet the urgent demand for this service as providers in a market economy. The businessmen who trade in women and force them to prostitute themselves indeed commit heavy crimes. And there are owners of brothels who pay reasonable salaries to their employees, including social insurance, and as patrons take care of drawers, painters and poets.

The big city with its trade fairs has always been a market place for venal love. In 1783, Johann Kaspar Riesbeck from Höchst anonymously published the "Briefe eines reisenden Franzosen über Deutschland an seinen Bruder in Paris" (Letters about Germany of a travelling Frenchman to his brother in Paris). There, one can read, for example: "There are many performances and concerts, a vauxhall, the nicest promenades, public dance halls and plenty of prostitutes. The last are more pushy than in any other German town. No man can walk along the promenades without being attacked by them. There are also different, although unprivileged public Venus temples, and some neighbouring villages are swarming with that kind of creatures, such as the village Bornheim, a part of the town, which has become famous for this commerce in whole Germany."

At Beate Uhse, branch Dr. Müller, where the girl from the pages 104/105 is waiting

Nowadays, the prostitutes do not attack anybody, and Bornheim has long lost its special fame. Today, the quarter all around the main station, **Bahnhofsviertel**, is Frankfurt's lust and vice district. It is not red light any more, but colourful neon signs which indicate that in these bars and brothels the guest can satisfy the lust of his eyes and all his other sensual organs. On Kaiserstraße, which leads from the main station into the city, Beate Uhse, Dr. Müller's Sex-World and other sex shops are all lined up one after the other. Only from time to time, the customers still dart bashfully into the shops that offer love equipment and everything bringing lust and joy – including professional consulting for men and women. The sex cinemas and blue movie theatres encourage the sexual drive of their visitors either in large halls or secret cabins. Side-streets, named after the rivers Mosel, Weser and Elbe, offer erotic establishments of all kind. Here, the busy clients take care for the maintenance of the jobs in the world's oldest profession.

Now, three spectacular cases of Frankfurt's criminal history shall be presented. The locations of the incidents have already been introduced on several walks.

A prostitute was the famous **Rosemarie Nitribitt**. Her name was Rosalie Marie Auguste, she was born in Ratingen near Düsseldorf on February 1, 1933 and killed in Frankfurt in the last days of October 1957. She was buried on the cemetery Nordfriedhof in Düsseldorf. As a child, she was badly off, and once she had become a teenager, she sold her body, earning good money. Then, she went to Frankfurt, where she worked as a waitress and a model, and finally again as a prostitute. She only got involved with rich men. And Rosemarie was successful in the times of the economic miracle. Managers, businessmen and politicians belonged to her clients. She drew attention when she was driving her Mercedes 190 SL all around Hauptwache or on Kaiserplatz, in front of the Frankfurter Hof. She was living in a nice flat in Stiftstraße 36 at the Eschenheimer Turm. That is the place where her dead body

The girl Rosemarie

was found on November 1, 1957. She had a laceration on her head and strangulation marks around her neck. Her notebook with the names of her clients had disappeared. One suspect was accused of having murdered the "demimondaine", but he was found not guilty in July 1960. The files were closed.

Speculations were flourishing. The press was searching for the truth. Wasn't it probable that rich and influential men had enough motive to fear the girl Rosemarie who could have blackmailed them? Was it impossible that these men should have used their influence to cover up the murder?

The journalist Erich Kuby published the bestseller "Rosemarie – des deutschen Wunders liebstes Kind" (Rosemarie), which was translated into many languages. In 1958, the screen adaptation "Das Mädchen Rosemarie" (A Girl Called Rosemarie) with Nadja Tiller was a money-spinner. In 1996, Bernd Eichinger shot a remake, showing stars in full force and Nina Hoss as Rosemarie. Both films were also broadcast on TV. Even today, half a century after her death, the figure of the girl Rosemarie still is wafted around by the secrets of a sinful legend.

Another girl whose story is related to sex and murder was **Susanna Margaretha Brand**. She was 23 years old. Her parents had already died, her sisters were married, and she was working as a servant in a guest-house. When

"Gretchen im Kerker" (Gretchen in the dungeon), etching by Johann Anton Ramboux, 1819

Close to the well at Hauptwache, Gretchen was beheaded

she met the servant of a Dutch merchant, she got all worked up after various glasses of wine, and according to her own words, could not resist. This was her first sexual intercourse and when she realised that she was pregnant, the servant had already left the town with his master. Gretchen hid her pregnancy and invented excuses for her condition. On August 1, 1771 she secretly gave birth to her child in the washhouse of the guesthouse. In order to hush up the disgrace of the illegitimate birth, she desperately killed the child and hid the corpse in the stables. Then, she dragged herself to one of her sisters' flat, who discovered the marks of a birth the next morning. The other sister was called, and Gretchen did not deny anything, but admitted the birth and the murder. Her sisters gave her some money that she could escape from town. She left Frankfurt through the gate Bockenheimer Tor, on the square Opernplatz, and went to Höchst, from where she left for Mainz by boat. Because she was still very weak, she couldn't start working. First, she came back to Höchst, then she returned to Frankfurt. Meanwhile, they had found the body of the dead child and were now searching for her by means of a "Wanted" circular. She was arrested at the Bockenheimer Tor and put behind bars in the tower Katharinenturm.

On January 7, 1772, she was sentenced to death, in spite of her lawyer's argumentation that she was an unlucky woman who regretted what she had done. The sentence reasoned that she "had wilfully and maliciously committed murder and therefore, according to the divine as well as the worldly laws, she had to be given her due punishment, serving as a disgusting example for others and sending her from life to death by sword…"

They erected the platform for the execution at Hauptwache. On January 14, 1772, Susanne Margarethe Brand was beheaded, surrounded by a gawking crowd, among them the young lawyer and poet Johann Wolfgang Goethe. Soon after that incident, Goethe started working on his "Faust", in which the tragedy of Gretchen found its poetic portrayal.

In 1998, on the occasion of Goethe's 249th birthday, the case Gretchen was newly heard before the judges and public prosecutors of the Hessian Court of Justice. The sentence: two years' probation.

The third case is not about murder, manslaughter and sex (not considering that success and money make sexy). It is about the "building tycoon" **Dr. Jürgen Schneider**. He was born in Frankfurt on April 30, 1934, being the son of a building contractor. He started as a bricklayer, then became a civil engineer and finally earned his doctorate in Political Sciences. Since 1963, he had worked in his father's company, but he left after a quarrel in 1982. The father is said to have told the banks not to give his son any credits.

The son successfully invested in real estates and soon owned more than 150 estates. Schneider mainly became famous for the restoration of historical buildings in Frankfurt, München, Leipzig and Berlin. An exceptional example in Frankfurt is the building "Fürstenhof" on the Gallusanlage near the theatre. The former hotel from 1901 had urgently needed a restoration, and Schneider turned it into an exclusive and representative business building.

One large project, profitably sold, financed the next. And the banks were willing to give him credits. In order to raise the amounts of the credits, he often faked the figures. Floors or usable areas were increased on the papers, pretending higher profits from rents, as happened in the case of the Zeilgalerie in Frankfurt. The poster at the building site, which could be read by anybody, indicated a usable area of 9,000 square metres. In the application for the corresponding credit, Schneider claimed 22,000 square metres. The lords in the twin towers belonging to Deutsche Bank did not check these numbers.

Fürstenhof

The twin towers of the Deutsche Bank

Unprofitable projects and the cooling down of the overheated real estate market caused deep rifts in the building of the Schneider system. He informed Deutsche Bank about his impending insolvency and went underground in 1994. The insolvency proceedings were opened. Schneider had more than DM 5 billion debts, nearly one quarter with the Deutsche Bank, whose then speaker of the board, Hilmar Kopper, called the amount "Peanuts", which as a result was declared the "Unwort", odd word, of the year.

In 1995, Schneider and his wife Claudia were arrested in Miami. On June 30, 1997 the regional court in Frankfurt opened the proceedings, during which the banks were found partially responsible, too. At least, they had offended against the credit and loan regulations of the Bank Act in many cases. Only Schneider was sentenced – to six years and nine months of imprisonment. In December 1999, he was released from prison, earlier than expected, for the time he had spent in prison on probation before the sentence had finally reduced his arrest. The building tycoon became a writer. He published his autobiography "Bekenntnisse eines Baulöwen" (Confessions of a building tycoon) and "Alle meine Häuser. Moderne Denkmale in Deutschland" (All my buildings. Modern monuments in Germany), and "Top oder Flop – Was gute Geschäfte von schlechten unterscheidet" (Top or flop – The difference between good and bad business). The profits are supposed to help the workmen who were harmed through the insolvency.

The satiric film by the director Carlo Rola was shown by the cinemas in 1996, later it was broadcast on TV. In the film, Jürgen Schneider is called Jochen Schuster, portrayed by Ulrich Mühe. The title of the film: "Peanuts – Die Bank zahlt alles" (Peanuts – The bank pays everything).

Service
*City map, addresses and offers,
boats, busses and trams*

The following pages should help the strollers and hikers when experiencing Frankfurt. They make walking easier and richer, turning the walk into a state of well-being.

Addresses and offers

In Frankfurt, the Tourismus+Congress GmbH Frankfurt on the Main, which has its service points, the tourist information offices, at Römer and at the main station, supplies people from Frankfurt and guests from all over the world with information, advice and support. There, you might also book hotels or tourist packages for your stay in Frankfurt.

Using the Frankfurt Card is an economical way of discovering and experiencing the town. You can buy it at the tourist information offices, but also in travel agencies, train stations, on the airport Fraport Terminal 1 Arrivals, hall B, and on the Internet. The Frankfurt Card includes a ticket for the public transport in the town's area, including journeys to the airport, and it gives you a discount of 25% on city sightseeing tours, 50% on admissions to 21 museums in Frankfurt, as well as to the Palm Garden, and 20% on the regular boat trips offered by KD Köln-Düsseldorfer Deutsche Rheinschifffahrt AG on Rhein and Mosel. Apart from that, you get free drinks, discounts or presents in several shops and restaurants.

Hauptbahnhof, main station

Tourismus+Congress GmbH Frankfurt am Main
Kaiserstr. 56
60329 Frankfurt am Main
Phone 0 69/21 23 87 03
Fax 0 69/21 23 07 76
info@tcf.frankfurt.de
www.frankfurt-tourismus.de

Tourist-Information Hauptbahnhof
Mon – Fri 8 am – 9 pm, Sat, Sun, holidays 9 am – 6 pm

Tourist-Information Römer
Römerberg 27
Mon – Fri 9.30 am – 5.30 pm,
Sat, Sun, holidays
10 am – 4 pm

Frankfurt Card
1-Day Ticket € 8.–
2-Day Ticket € 12.–

25 out of the numerous museums in Frankfurt, not only on the Museums' Bank, can be visited for a better price when using the Museumsufer-Card and the Museumsufer-Ticket. The card is a annual-season ticket that gives you free entrance to these museums, also during the museums' night, "Museumsnacht", and during the Museums' Bank Festival, "Museumsuferfest". Furthermore, you get the art magazine Artkaleidoscope three times a year.

The Museumsufer-Ticket is a 2-day ticket, which allows free entrance to these museums and, additionally, the nature museum Senckenberg; only if there is a special exhibition, for which the admission lies at € 5 and more, you have to pay the reduced fee.

Museumsufer-Card
€ 65.–, reduced € 33.–,
family card € 120.–

Museumsufer-Ticket
€ 12.–, reduced € 6.–,
family ticket € 20.–

Available at the museums, at the tourist information offices, at „Frankfurt Ticket" in the underground floor at Hauptwache, and on the phone at k/c/e Marketing Services
0 69/97 46 02 30,
www.museumsufercard.de

Guided Tours in Frankfurt

Apart from sightseeing tours, Tourismus+Congress GmbH Frankfurt am Main also organises informative and entertaining guided walks for groups. The walks "Frankfurt all along the Main" and "Historical Frankfurt" take about 2 hours, whereas the walk "History and presence" lasts three hours. There are other thematic tours, such as "Frankfurt as a financial, economic and European metropolis", "Frankfurt and its cider, the Ebbelwei", "Architecture in Frankfurt", "The Museums' Bank", "The Jewish Frankfurt", "On Goethe's tracks", "Famous and forgotten women from Frankfurt", "Historical crime story", "Arts in public places". The tours "The church Paulskirche and its parliament" and "The emperors' hall Kaisersaal in the town hall Römer" take 45 minutes each. Children at the age of primary school can take part in the walk "Emperors, walls, towers".

Guided tours can also be booked at the Kulturothek, which organises presentations and sells presents from Frankfurt, too.

Kulturothek
An der Kleinmarkthalle 7
60311 Frankfurt am Main
Phone 0 69/28 10 10
Fax 0 69/28 10 70

info@kulturothek.de
www.kulturothek.de
Business hours
Mon – Fri 10 am – 4 pm,
Sat 11 am – 2 pm

Stefanie Reimann, M.A., born and grown up in Frankfurt, has studied here, in Berlin, Granada and Toronto. She has been organising travels and guided tours in English and German through Frankfurt, and she has also attended to official delegations that had come to Frankfurt. Her daughter Charlotte made her think of guided tours for children, the groups consisting of no more than 25 children and chaperons. The walks and rallies can be arranged individually.

Stefanie Reimann 4 Kids

"The town and the river", that is the name of one rally with questionnaire and city map; length: 1.5 hours, age recommendation: 8 years and older. On the rally "Römerberg" the children explore the alleys all around the hill by means of tape measures, city map and questionnaire; length: 1.5 hours, age recommendation: 10 years and older. When walking through the "Goethe House", children become poets and the best will be awarded prizes; length: 1.5 hours, age: 10 years and older. The exploration of the "Towers" deals with old buildings as well as modern skyscrapers. The children will look down at the towers from the famous Maintower, which is about 200 metres high; length: 2 hours, age: 6 years and older. "Money and trade" is the name of a walk from Römerberg through the quarter of the banks to the bourse; length: 1 to 2 hours; 8 years and older. A visit at bull, bear, DAX and "Börse", the bourse, also explains what floor trade is about; length: 45 minutes, 8 years and older. "Rascals, rogues, crooks" is a walk through the history of crime; length: 1 to 2 hours, 8 years and older.

Frankfurt 4 Kids
Stefanie Reimann info@frankfurt4kids.de
Phone 069/78 98 79 98 www.frankfurt4kids.de

Setting sail for pleasure

Those who want to make a pleasurable rest on their walks through the town can go to Eiserner Steg, the footbridge over the Main. This is the place where the white excursion boats start. Every day from noon on, the boats start hourly for a small cruise, passing the town's skyline towards the mill Gerbermühle or downriver to Griesheim. In the evenings, one can get a Riversight Dinner; during the cruise the organiser offers a four-course menu with live music. The nice boats of the shipping company Primus take you to Seligenstadt, Aschaffenburg, Bingen on the Rhein, Rüdesheim and the Loreley, to Worms and Heidelberg.

Primus-Linie	60311 Frankfurt am Main
Frankfurter	Phone 0 69/1 33 83 70
Personenschifffahrt	Fax 0 69/28 47 98
Anton Nauheimer GmbH	mail@primus-linie.de
Mainkai 36	www.primus-linie.de

Nostalgia on rails

The trains of the historical railway stop at the footbridge Eiserner Steg, the central station, and go all along the banks of the river Main – to the east until Mainkur, to the west until Griesheim. Usually, the nostalgic trains are pulled by the steam locomotive 52 4867 from the year 1943.

Historic Railway
Postfach 90 03 45
60443 Frankfurt am Main
Phone 0 69/43 60 93
info@HistorischeEisen-
bahnFrankfurt.de

www.HistorischeEisenbahn-
Frankfurt.de
Schedule
last Sun March – June,
Sept – Nov, Santa Claus
Trains in Dec

Ebbelwei Express

When using the colourfully-painted vintage tram for your journey, the offered drink – Ebbelwei, apple juice or water – as well as some salty biscuits are already included. The sightseeing tours start at the zoo, go to Römer/Paulskirche, main station, exhibition hall, to Sachsenhausen, Südbahnhof and back to the zoo. The funny journey takes one hour and 10 minutes.

Ebbelwei-Expreß
VGF Verkehrsgesellschaft
Frankfurt am Main
Kurt-Schumacher-Str. 10
60311 Frankfurt am Main
Phone 0 69/21 32 24 25
Fax 0 69/21 32 27 27

info@vgf-ffm.de
www.vgf-ffm.de
Schedule
Sat, Sun, holidays from
1.30 pm
Tickets
€ 5.–, children € 2.50

Good on the way with RMV

The transport company VGF Frankfurt am Main belongs to the traffic association RMV Rhein-Main Verkehrsverbund, both construct a dense network of good traffic connections all over the region. And in Frankfurt, trams, underground and regional trains as well as busses take care that walkers and hikers reach the starting points of their walks easily and that they will get back safe and sound. Apart from single tickets, there are also group tickets, day tickets, as well as weekly, monthly and annual season tickets. On your inquiry, you will get friendly information about time tables, prices and other details.

RMV Rhein-Main-Verkehrsverbund GmbH
Alte Bleiche 5
65719 Hofheim am Taunus
Phone 0 61 92/29 40

Fax 0 61 92/29 49 00
Information and tips:
Hotline 0 18 05/7 68 46 36
WAP-Service: wap.rmv.de
www.rmv.de

traffiQ Frankfurt am Main
Verkehrsinsel
An der Hauptwache
Zeil 129
60313 Frankfurt am Main
Phone 0 69/2 12 03
Fax 0 69/21 22 33 71

Hotline 0 18 05/06 99 60
info@cgf-ffm.de
www.traffiQ.de
Business hours
Mon – Fri 9 am – 8 pm,
Sat 9.30 am – 6 pm

Index of Photographs:

Klaus Dill   37 (from: Klaus Dill "Kunst fürs Kino", Heider Verlag/Henschel Verlag, 2002), 85 (from: Klaus Dill „Ein Künstlerleben für Literatur und Film", Heider Verlag/Societäts-Verlag, 2004)
Frankfurt 4 Kids   121
Frankfurter Feldbahnmuseum, photo Karl Wolf (from: "Hessen für Eisenbahnfreunde", Societäts-Verlag)
"Frankfurter Wirtschaftswunderkinder. Die Mainmetropole in den 50er Jahren" by Sabine Börchers, Societäts-Verlag, 2006)   09
Frankfurter Goethe-Museum/Otani University Museum   110 (from: Catalogue "Goethes Faust. Verwandlungen eines Hexenmeisters", 2005)
GrünGürtel Frankfurt, Umweltamt   92, 93 (from: "GrünGürtel Frankfurt" und "Hinter Frankfurt das Meer. Literarische Entdeckungen des GrünGürtels", Societäts-Verlag, 2005)
Höchster Porzellan-Manufaktur   99
Jüdisches Museum Frankfurt   57, 62 (from: Catalogue "Moritz Daniel Oppenheim", 2000)
Museum Giersch   27 (from: Catalogue "Bilder aus dem Leben. Genremalerei im Rhein-Main-Gebiet", 2005)
"Der Palmengarten. Ein Führer durch Frankfurts Grünoase" by Beate Taudte-Repp, Societäts-Verlag, 2005   83
RMV Rhein-Main-Verkehrsverbund GmbH   125, 127ff
© Stadtvermessungsamt Frankfurt am Main, 2006, Liz.-Nr.: 6233-3306-D   Vorsatz, 11, 21, 30, 49, 57, 68, 80, 107
Das Städel   32, 33, 34
traffiQ Frankfurt am Main   124
All other photographs: Eberhard Urban

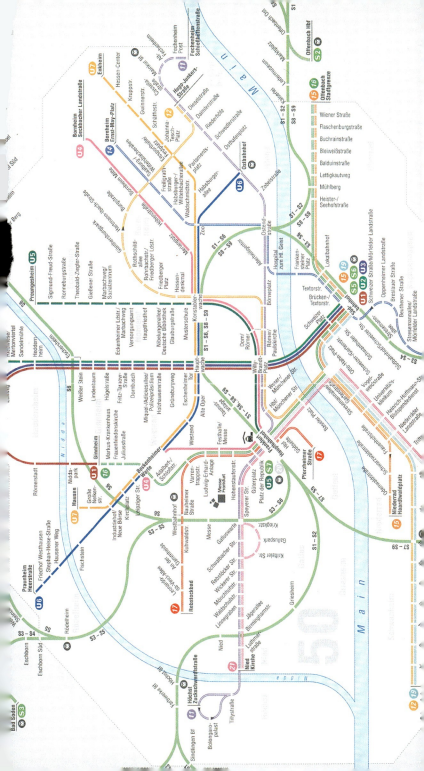

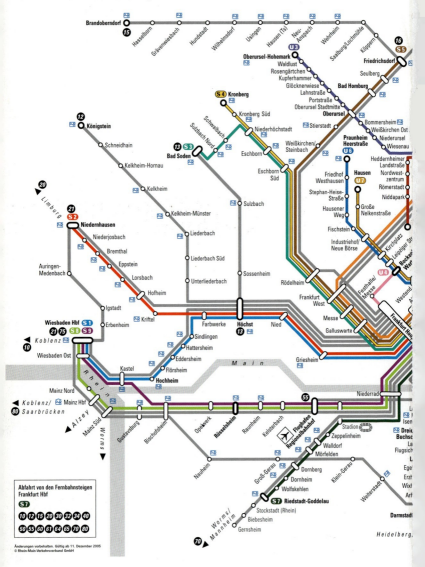